W9-DGC-245

GREAT BRITAIN & HANOVER

SOME ASPECTS OF THE PERSONAL UNION

BEING THE FORD LECTURES
DELIVERED IN THE UNIVERSITY OF OXFORD
HILARY TERM, 1899

BY

ADOLPHUS WILLIAM WARD, LITT.D.

HASKELL HOUSE PUBLISHERS Ltd.

Publishers of Scarce Scholarly Books

NEW YORK, N. Y. 10012

1971

First Published 1899

HASKELL HOUSE PUBLISHERS Ltd.
Publishers of Scarce Scholarly Books
280 LAFAYETTE STREET
NEW YORK. N. Y. 10012'

Library of Congress Catalog Card Number: 68-25282

Standard Book Number 8383-0252-1

Printed in the United States of America

PREFACE

— ·•· —

THE subject of the relations between Great Britain and Hanover has long seemed to me to deserve a more special study than has hitherto been devoted to it. But no enquiry into these relations can be considered in any sense complete, unless it should include a careful examination of the documentary evidence preserved at Hanover, both in the Archives of the Ministry, and in those of the London Chancery. It was therefore with some hesitation that I suggested this subject for the course which I had the honour of being invited to deliver at Oxford in the academical year 1898–99; since my engagements made it impossible for me to undertake the requisite inspection within the time at my disposal. On the whole, however, I thought that a useful purpose might be served by an attempt to bring certain aspects of the theme under the notice of hearers interested in this period of history, and that, possibly, younger or more competent hands might thus be induced at one point or another to take up the thread. For myself, I had no choice but to confine my comments mainly, though not altogether, to the reigns of George I and II, and this again made it necessary that the first of my lectures should largely occupy itself with the history of the House of Bruns-

wick before the accession of the Elector George Lewis
to the British throne.   I trust that these introductory
pages may not be considered superfluous, if they
throw any light upon the policy of the earlier Hanoverian reigns, derived from a study of the historical
traditions of the dynasty, and more especially of its
political action from the Peace of Westphalia to the
Peace of Utrecht.

I desire here to repeat my thanks to Dr. R. Doebner,
Archivist of State, &c., for having, by the information
which he was kind enough to transmit to me, enabled
me to explain the actual working of the Hanoverian
system of government, more especially as to the
relations between the territorial sovereign and the
higher ministerial authorities.

These lectures had been written, and in the fifth
of the series I had already largely availed myself of
the researches of M. Richard Waddington in his
Louis XV et le Renversement des Alliances (1754–56),
when he was so courteous as to allow me to
peruse the proof-sheets of the chapter on Kloster
Zeven in his forthcoming continuation of his important
political narrative.   I was thus enabled to rewrite so
much of my sixth lecture as refers to the Capitulation and its reception in England, although I have
not yet had the satisfaction of reading the remainder
of the expected volume.

                                   A. W. WARD.

KENSINGTON, *March* 24, 1899.

P.S. Since these lines were written, M. Waddington's *La Guerre de Sept Ans, Les Débuts* has appeared
in print.

CONTENTS

—•+•—

GREAT BRITAIN AND HANOVER

—•—

LECTURE I

INTRODUCTORY

THE Personal Union between Great Britain and Hanover, of which in the present short course of lectures I propose to consider some of the aspects, lasted, as you are aware, for nearly a century and a quarter. It came to an end, as there is even less need of reminding you, with Her present Majesty's accession to a throne happily barred against her accession by no public or private law or usage. Prince Bismarck, in the very remarkable chapter on ' Dynasties and Peoples' included in his *Reflections and Recollections*[1], may or may not be mistaken as to the nature of the tie between the British people and the dynasty now occupying its throne. But he most assuredly underestimates the degree in which the reign of Queen Victoria has been propitious to the conservation and renewal of the spirit that sustains the monarchical form of government in these islands, and in the empire of which they form the centre.

Now, throughout the long term of its endurance, the union of which we are about to treat remained a Personal Union pure and simple, in the strictest sense of a term

[1] Vol. i. ch. 13.

which, like many other expressions taken over by science from practice, lends itself to a good deal of shading-off, both in the way of formal use and in that of substantial significance. Into the political connexion between Great Britain and Hanover there entered no element of federal relations of any sort or kind. As has been pointed out by the most recent enquirer into the *modus vivendi* (if I may so call it) between the partners in this connexion, it was nothing more than an official flourish of style indulged in on the one side, but left quite unreciprocated on the other, when the Electors of Brunswick-Lüneburg, in their rescripts to their Hanoverian subjects, designated themselves as Kings of Great Britain. France, and Ireland, or afterwards as Sovereigns of the United Kingdom, and when their electoral officials made mention in their titulatures of the higher foreign dignity of their territorial princes[1]. But not only were the relations between the two political communities, whose conditions of life and progress could not fail to be more or less affected by their union under the rule of the same sovereign, unmarked by any co-ordination or subordination of rights or claims implying legalised interdependence. No contiguity of frontier, no joint historical experience—often a far more effective agent of political consolidation than the closest kinship of race—helped to blend their respective interests and aspirations, or to efface the contrasts in their political life. Doubtless they thus likewise avoided the risk of direct collisions such as have often sprung from the jealousies and rivalries between neighbour populations connected by similar ties,—between their political conceptions, their religious beliefs,

[1] Speaking of themselves as 'Königlich Grossbritannische, Kurfürstlich Braunschweig-Lüneburgsche' or (after 1814) 'Königlich Grossbritannisch-Hannoversche' councillors or magistrates. See E. von Meier, *Hannoversche Verfassungs- und Verwaltungsgeschichte*, vol. i. (Leipzig, 1898), p. 122.

and their very forms of speech. We should not need to go
far afield in order to find examples of personal unions
between States which have led—some to real political union
and national amalgamation, others to passionate strife and
lacerating disrupture. But it would hardly be worth while
to linger over instances so familiar. Perhaps the most
striking example of a personal union pure and simple—
although in its duration more transitory than that of which
I am asking you to note some of the aspects, and in its
formal conditions absolutely unique—was that into which
Great Britain herself entered as a result of the Revolution
of 1688. The union brought about by the statecraft of
William III of Orange, and represented by him in his own
person, went far towards combining into a single mighty
force the capabilities and resources of two great polities
whom, a generation earlier, some of the leaders of the English
Commonwealth had dreamt of fusing into a single State[1].
If William III so far found his account in the personal
union effected by him that, according to a contemporary
saying, though but a Stadholder in England he was a King
at home, the liberties of the United Provinces underwent
at most a temporary eclipse[2]; nor was it till a later day
that, for the preservation of their existence, they paid the
price of the downfall of their political importance. In the
long run, however, the predominance of the monarchical
partner in the time-honoured conjunction of the Maritime
Powers came to be accepted as a fact by friend and by foe
alike. Even in matters commercial the reign of William III
marks the beginning of the ascendancy of his adopted over

[1] Cf. Gardiner, *History of the Commonwealth and Protectorate,*
vol. i. pp. 356 seq.; vol. ii. p. 344.
[2] For a very strong statement as to the deminution of political rights
suffered by the Provinces under William's government, see Pontalis,
John de Witt (English translation, 1885), vol. ii. p. 511.

his native country, although after his death something like half a century was to pass before Dutch commerce could be definitively pronounced to have lost its supremacy.

The rumour was absolutely false which, quite towards the close of William III's reign, so greatly perturbed the Princess Anne and her friends, that the King intended the House of Hanover to succeed to the English throne immediately upon his own decease ; and Anne's own reign delayed during twelve eventful years the repetition, under wholly different conditions, of the experiment tried by William III in his own person.   In discussing the Personal Union between Great Britain and Hanover under our male sovereigns of the House of Guelph, I shall ask you to devote to the reigns of George I and George II a measure of attention which you will scarcely, under the circumstances, judge to be disproportionate.   And this, not only because of the denunciations, in part at least beyond all question clap-trap, into which most of our leading politicians in these reigns, as well as the great body of public opinion at various stages in their course, launched forth against Hanover and Hanoverian influence.   Manifestly, if the electoral dynasty brought with it from the banks of Leine and Aller to our shores any distinctive traditions, principles or methods, these must have found their fullest and most direct expression under its earliest representatives on the acquired throne ; and as is well known the most notable feature in the character of our first two Hanoverian sovereigns was tenaciousness.   George I was crowned king at the age of fifty-four—an age at which few men are apt to change either principles of thought or habits of action, least of all one in whom a glacial reserve of manner covered a self-centred disposition and a strong will.   The political nurture of this prince had intimately associated him with a group of European soldiers and statesmen in which King William III's

was incontestably the foremost figure, but which included
a few Englishmen, with Dutchmen, Germans, and French
Huguenots, worthy of his familiarity and equal to his trust.
The succession, failing issue from Anne, of the House of
Hanover to the thrones of Great Britain and Ireland, had
gradually come to form an integral part of the political system
or programme of these far-sighted reasoners and reckoners.
Our first Hanoverian king carried with him into his new
dominions not only the lessons and traditions which he had
derived from this training, but certain highly intelligent dis-
ciples of the school which it had bred, and the fixity of whose
tenets signally contrasts with the more fluctuating views and
purposes of many among the leaders of contemporary English
political—that is to say, parliamentary—life. Moreover,
King George I was never at the pains to conceal the fact
that he had become ruler of these islands by force of circumstances rather than by his own choice ; nor, as is well known,
was it ever in his opinion worth his while to take the first
step towards becoming an Englishman by acquiring the use
of the language spoken by his English subjects. It would
certainly seem, as I may note by the way, without pre-
tending that a call for reciprocity existed in the matter, as if
such of these subjects as were brought into close personal
relations with him, had taken quite as little trouble on their
side to learn the native tongue of their prince ; and this complete indifference of English courtiers and statesmen to a
tongue without some knowledge of which they could not
expect to penetrate far into the Hanoverian interests of their
sovereigns, continued without much change under George II [1].

[1] Lord Hervey (*Memoirs of the Reign of George II*, ed. Croker.
1884, vol. ii. p. 389) mentions the *naïve* suggestion that the Princess
Augusta of Saxe-Gotha, when on the point of marrying Frederick Prince
of Wales, might spare herself the trouble of learning German, since
'most people in England' would be sure to speak German as well as

In other respects, the general character of the personal relations between king and people promised to improve when
George II succeeded to his father. 'I am very much
mistaken,' wrote Bothmer (who perhaps contributed more
than any other servant of the House of Hanover to its establishment upon the British throne), 'if he has not more inclination for this crown than the Elector his father; but this had
better remain between ourselves, since it would not do for our
English friends to be aware of our indifference on this head [1].'
Although, however, neither in disposition nor in temperament
George II altogether resembled his predecessor, and although
the relative stability of his throne could not but react upon
his view of his own position as its occupant,—yet the political
and moral influences to which father and son had been
severally subjected were not essentially dissimilar, and their

they spoke English; which conjecture, he says, was 'so well founded
that I believe there were not three natives in England that understood
one word of German better than in the reign of Queen Anne.' Lord
Hervey's father, the first Earl of Bristol, places on record (see his
Diary, Wells, 1894, pp. 73, 77) the French speech which he made to
George I, at St. James' on October 26, 1722, and a similar speech
addressed by him to George II, at Leicester Fields House in 1747.
Sir Robert Walpole is stated to have preferred to address King George I
in such Latin as he could muster. It is an equally familiar fact that
among the ministers of George II, Lord Carteret, who was a most
accomplished modern linguist as well as a genuine classical scholar,
owed the personal influence which he secured over the King in no
small measure to the quite exceptional circumstance of his own
knowledge of German. In his recent address on *Literary Statesmen*
(November 25, 1898), Lord Rosebery, according to the *Times* report,
pointed out that, while Carteret thus excelled, 'perhaps the only startling
deficiency in Chesterfield's intellectual equipment was his unaccountable
ignorance of the mother-tongue of that Hanoverian dynasty which he
was so anxious to serve.'

[1] See the letter from Bothmer to Ilten, in which the former, as early
as the spring of 1701, advocated a sojourn in England by the Electoral
Prince, afterwards King George II, *ap.* Bodemann, *J. H. von Ilten*
(Hanover, 1879), p. 133.

principles both of public government and of private conduct
harmonised more thoroughly than the sentiments entertained
by them for one another might have seemed to render likely.
Perhaps, although inordinately ambitious, and inflated by
a sense of individual importance superfluous to his predecessor's stolid sense of dignity, George II was, by the
constitution of his mind as well as through the force of
circumstances, less completely master of his aims than
George I. His acumen as an observer both of men and of
measures, coupled with an extravagant fondness for administrative detail, stimulated his interest in the affairs of his
kingdom as well as of his electorate. But, apart from the
fact that he had grown into manhood long before his first
actual arrival in England (when he was already in his thirty-
first year), he lacked the grasp of mind—some may prefer to
call it the power of imagination—which would have enabled
him to understand the opportunities as well as the difficulties
of his position ; nor was his excess of self-will in the end proof
against either cajolery or firmness. But his dynastic preferences
and prejudices were quite as eager as his father's had been
before him, and, being more vehement in expression, they
asserted themselves more patently, though they were less
continuously seconded by responsible British statesmanship.
Thus in the reigns of our first two Georges the conditions
of conflict between English and Hanoverian interests and
influences were, in some measure at least, homogeneous
though not identical. All this was changed with the commencement of the long reign of George III, who made appeal
to the loyalty of his English subjects as himself an Englishman born and bred, and who during his lifetime never set
foot in his Hanoverian Electorate. Although as a matter of
fact the foremost of the Hanoverian counsellors of the Crown
in George II's reign only attained to the height of ministerial
power under his successor, yet with the close of the Seven

Years' War the direct political importance of the connexion
between the two countries came, except incidentally, to a long
stop. More than forty years had gone by before the territorial interests of the Elector and the Electorate of Hanover,
imperilled in turn by the friendship and by the hostility
between France and Prussia, again played an important part
in conflicts directly affecting the interests of Great Britain as
a great European Power. To these events and transactions
brief reference will be made in a concluding lecture ; but it
will be barely possible to glance at ideas of ulterior developements, which, had effect been given to them at the close of
the Napoleonic era, might have added a new and unprecedented significance to the last phase of the history of the
Personal Union.

While, therefore, except towards the close of the actual endurance of that Union, few changes will require notice in those
formal relations between the two governments which i propose to describe in outline in my second lecture, it will be
readily allowed that such importance as the connexion
possesses for our political history mainly attaches itself to the
first two Hanoverian reigns, and afterwards to certain passages
of the Napoleonic epoch. You will not, I hope, desire me
to follow the example of certain English historical writers
who have previously addressed themselves to this subject, and
to ignore the effects of the Personal Union upon the fortunes
of the less of the two political bodies concerned in it. Nor
can I think that, in dwelling in its turn upon this side of my
theme, I shall be untrue to the spirit of my duties as a lecturer
in English history. The Personal Union with Hanover entailed upon our country duties not to be shaken off either by
clamour or by formal disclaimers, but needing definition, and
(as is inevitable in politics) a frequent revision of definition,
under the light of facts. Where the consequences of that Union
were left to wreak themselves as they might upon the weaker

partner, the stronger remained accountable to a tribunal which declines to accept expediency as a conclusive plea.

It forms no part of my present purpose to recall the circumstances of the Succession of the House of Hanover to the British throne, or to discuss the transactions, of which to this day no altogether satisfactory history has yet been composed, that led up to a consummation of unmistakeable advantage to the progress of our national life. On the other hand, it will, I think, be useful to devote the remainder of this opening lecture to a rapid survey of so much—and no more—of the history of the House of Hanover before the Succession as may serve to throw light upon dynastic traditions, ideas, and tendencies, of which the influence remains traceable in the course of British political history at all events during the first two Hanoverian reigns.

Neither the antiquities of the House of Brunswick, on which Gibbon wrote a dissertation unfortunately left uncompleted, nor the wider researches of Leibniz into the origin of the House of Guelph, must detain us on the threshold. Our great historian, in his inimitable way, remarks that ' an English subject may be prompted, by a just and liberal curiosity, to investigate the origin and story of the House of Brunswick, which, after an alliance with the daughter of our kings, has been called by the voice of a free people to the legal inheritance of the crown.' Gibbon, who had a right to profess a love for Italy such as he cherished for no other foreign country, was more particularly attracted by that portion of his theme which was concerned with the connexion between the House of Este and the House of Brunswick, definitively established by the researches of Leibniz. Thus, while the English summary brought down the fortunes of the Italian House to its last male representative Hercules III, Duke of Modena, a contemporary of the writer, it carried the history of the German no further than the latter part of the twelfth

century,—the period when its greatness seemed to have
reached its highest pitch in the sway of Henry the Lion, and
to have ended for ever with his downfall. The monumental
work of Leibniz, on a portion of whose labours Gibbon's
essay was based, was, after its design had been expanded
(something in the fashion of the plan of Gibbon's own
masterpiece), again reduced to narrower chronological limits,
so far as Leibniz' own share in it was concerned. He had
very nearly reached the year 1024, and the death of the last
Saxon Emperor Henry II, which he had proposed to himself as his *finis chartae*, when his own indefatigable hand was
stayed by death. The Elector Ernest Augustus, to whom
Leibniz afterwards devoted a monograph, and the entire
House of Brunswick-Lüneburg, of which he had been named
the historiographer, had approved of his vast scheme of
enlarging the Annals of that House into those of the Western
Empire from the era of Charles the Great onwards, while constantly keeping in view the Brunswick line and its dominions.
But George I had not inherited together with the clearness
the liberality of mind that distinguished his mother the
Electress Sophia, Leibniz' faithful friend ; and he had no
patience with the protraction of the great author's preparations for his work, which went on for nearly a quarter of a
century before, at his death, he left his intended share of it in
a condition very near completeness. Nor, indeed, was it
even then published in full as he had left it behind him,—
a consummation not reached till 1843, when another
historiographer of the House of Brunswick-Lüneburg, the
editor of the *Monumenta Germaniae*, at last paid this debt to
the historical services of the great writer who had preceded
him in both capacities. In the Preface to his edition of the
Annales, Pertz briefly adverts to the ignoble pressure put by
George I and his ministers upon their illustrious dependant ;
but the story has since been supplemented from Leibniz'

correspondence, most recently from that with the minister Bernstorff[1]. It forms a rather painful episode in the history—not a very overflowing one—of the relations between the House of Hanover and literature; nor, in view of what Leibniz in this instance actually accomplished, can the great thinker's insatiable desire to exhaust any scientific enquiry in which he had engaged be pleaded in extenuation of the discourtesies inflicted upon him. Moreover, as a publicist Leibniz was not less prompt than he was deliberate as a historiographer,—a title which he seems at times to have sought, and at other times to have disdained[2]. His political intelligence, capable of such a design as the aversion of a European war by means of a French invasion of Egypt[3], could condescend to the compilation of a long treatise proving that princes of the empire not possessed of the electoral dignity were entitled to the same measure of sovereign rights as that belonging to the dukes of Modena and Mantua, and take part in the controversy as to precedence between the Banner of the Empire

---

[1] See *Leibnizen's Briefwechsel mit dem Minister von Bernstorff*, &c. Herausgegeben von Dr. R. Doebner (Hanover, 1882).

[2] Apart from his post in the Hanoverian service, Leibniz was at different times anxious to be appointed historiographer of Brandenburg and of England, and seems also to have thought of occupying a similar position at Vienna. (Bothmer writes to Robethon, August 11, 1716 (*Robethon Papers*, vol. iii. p. 21), that Leibniz desires the title of historiographer of England, and that he would deserve it, if he would finish the history of the House of Brunswick, on which head Stanhope might do well to give him a hint.) But in 1699 he had protested to the Duchess of Celle, that he 'had never taken, and could never take, the position of historiographer.' It was only, he asserted, in the course of his endeavour to ascertain the rights of the House of Brunswick, that it became his task to occupy himself incidentally with its history. (See *Nachträge zu Leibnizen's Briefen an Bernstorff*, &c., in *Zeitschrift des historischen Vereins für Niedersachsen*, Jahrgang 1890, p. 140.)

[3] As to this curious project (1671), see Guhrauer, *Leibnitz* (Breslau, 1846), vol. i. pp. 92 seqq.

borne by Hanover, and 'he Banner of Battle appertaining to
Württemberg.   The House of Hanover had no second advo-
cate of its rights and claims equipped with such historical
knowledge and literary ability as his ; nor was it his fault if
that House made light of the opportunity of blending his
fame with its own [1].

A man of letters of another sort, William Whitehead, the
harmless poet-laureate of George III's days, whom Johnson
censured so severely for the grand nonsense of his birthday
odes, in one of these rather unexpectedly introduces a tenth-
century ancestor of the House of Guelph.   Him, when about

---

[1] There is no very strong temptation to enlarge upon the earlier
relations between the House of Hanover and our own national literature.
It was not the fault of that House that its praises were sung by Elkanah
Settle in his *Eusebia Triumphans*, or *The Hanover Succession* (1704) ;
nor is it to be blamed because its unsophisticated attitude towards the
progress of poësy was satirised by Pope, because (as Dr. Courthope has
shown) the wits thought it incumbent upon them to range themselves
on the side of the opposition.   The true laureate of our early Hanoverian
kings was not Colley Cibber (though he was a German by birth) or any
of his successors, but the illustrious musician, whom England really
owes to Hanover, but to whose greatest achievements she in her turn
proved no grudging step-mother.   Handel, who in his childhood had
first attracted wider attention, on being taken to the Court of George I's
accomplished sister Sophia Charlotte, at Berlin, was admitted into the
Hanoverian service at Venice in 1709, and was in the same year from
Hanover granted leave for his first visit to London.   After the accession
of George I he was, though a more serious defaulter than Leibniz, more
graciously forgiven, and taken back into favour.   The flights of his muse
upon the banks of the Thames delighted George I, as the royal barge
glided down stream ; he composed the coronation anthems for George II
and the hymns of mourning on the death of Queen Caroline ; he celebrated what, in the eyes of the victor, was the greatest glory of the reign
in the *Dettingen Te Deum*, and honoured the hero of Culloden by
symbolising his success in the patriotic achievements of *Judas Maccabaeus*.
Klopstock (see his ode *Wir und Sie*, 1766) might well take pride in
Germany's gift to England of Handel's music ; but he should have
abstained from throwing in Kneller's uninspired art.

to cross into Germany, the genius of the Julian Alps invites
to fix his 'visual nerve'—

> ' Where, crown'd with rocks grotesque and steep,
> The white isle rises o'er the deep,
> There Glory rests [1].'

No such thought is, however, likely to have haunted even
the imagination of Henry the Lion at an epoch when his
territorial power reached from the German Ocean to the
mountains of the Tyrol, and from the Baltic to the Adriatic.
As it chanced, the good word of an English king—the far-
sighted Henry II—helped to induce the Emperor Frederick
Barbarossa to mitigate the severity of the treatment which
he had intended to inflict upon the great vassal before whom
a few years earlier he had abased himself in vain. Thus there
were preserved to Henry and his descendants the lands between Weser and Elbe, whence after more than five cen-
turies one of these descendants set forth to mount the British
throne. In 1235 Henry the Lion's grandson, Otto the
Child, surrendered all these territories, which after being
subdivided had been again united in his person, into the
hands of the Emperor Frederick II. and received them
back from him as an imperial fief under the name of the
Duchy of Brunswick. Since, in the deed of imperial investiture, the new duchy was attached to the city of Brunswick
and the castle of Lüneburg, the successors of Otto called
themselves Dukes of Brunswick, at other times of Brunswick-
Lüneburg, or Dukes of Brunswick and Lords of Lüneburg :
and 'Brunswick' or 'Brunswick-Lüneburg' henceforth was
and remained the proper style of the house in its entirety.
Some time after the death of Otto the Child his two elder
sons proceeded to a repartition of the paternal inheritance ;

[1] William Whitehead's *Ode on His Majesty's Birthday*, November 10,
1758.

and this particular distribution of the Brunswick-Lüneburg dominions was never undone, and has, in consequence of the annexation of Hanover to the Prussian monarchy, remained in force ever since the death, in 1884, of the last sovereign Duke of Brunswick[1]. No similar fixity attended the innumerable partitions and subdivisions that complicate the annals of the Old, Middle, and New Houses of Brunswick and Lüneburg, to an extent almost unparalleled even in the history of German dynasties, which George II used to upbraid Englishmen at his Court for being so slow to master. Over these complications I have not the least wish to waste your time; but, in view of the later history of the house of Brunswick in particular, it is worth pointing out that these repeated partitions, which weakened so many princely houses and prolonged the hopelessness of national disunion, were deeply rooted in Germanic law and usage. Only quite gradually— from the fourteenth century onwards, but with little immediate effect upon the simplification of the territorial map of the Empire—this system was modified by special laws of *inalienability* and *indivisibility* established for themselves by particular princely families. Primogeniture came later, and as is shown in the instance of the Hanoverian line, was most bitterly resisted by the interests affected. In the Reformation period a union of government, or at least a systematic co-operation, between the several branches of the House of Guelph, might have raised that House to an exceptional height of power and influence in Germany. In this period, as you are aware, the secularisation of the great ecclesiastical sees materially contributed to swell the dominions of divers temporal princes;

---

[1] A reunion would have taken place between Brunswick on the one hand and Lüneburg and Calenberg (Hanover)—the diminished possessions of the younger line—on the other, had not the proposals made in this sense after Sadowa been rejected in deference to the sagacious advice of Bismarck. (See *u. s.*, vol. ii. p. 72.)

and in the early years of the sixteenth century nearly all the richest bishoprics of this region of Germany,—Paderborn, *Osnabrück*, Münster, *Verden* and *Bremen*,—fell in turn into Guelph hands. Hildesheim alone, the venerable foundation of Lewis the Pious, saved a remnant of its domains out of the clutches of the Brunswick dukes, whom its bishop had at first defeated in the open field with the aid of their Lüneburg kinsmen. The interests of the dynasty thus coincided with the impulses of the population; nor could personal divergences, due to various motives, in after times shake the attachment of the Guelphs to a sober and tolerant Lutheranism. I shall briefly advert further on to the principles and policy in matters ecclesiastical of our earlier Hanoverian Kings, and need only remind you at present that in them the Lutheran traditions of their House had been interfused in peculiar fashion both with an unmistakeable vein of rationalism, and with a spirit of tolerance alike bequeathed to her descendants and younger companions by the Electress Sophia. In some of the more critical stages, however, of its history, the Reformation had not only divided the Guelphs against one another, but had driven into temporary exile its violent adversary Duke Henry of Brunswick, the 'evil Hal' of Luther's brutal invective. Again, in the years preceding the Thirty Years' War, and in those covering its earlier half, a consistently combined action between the two main divisions of the House might, in conformity with the sentiments of their subjects, have established a strong bulwark of the Protestant cause in the German North-West, and successfully withstood the hordes that, in the name of the ruler of the Empire, were devastating this part of it almost like another Palatinate. But the politics of the Brunswick branch were Imperialist already in the time before the War, when the House of Austria had no more constant friend and no more assiduous adviser than Duke Henry Julius. His memorable activity was divided between high politics abroad, civic struggles at home, and the literary occupations and diversions which make him so fascinating a figure to students of both the English and the German drama. But neither his untiring diplomacy, nor the timorous shifts of his successor Frederick Ulric, averted from the Brunswick-Lüneburg dominions the awful scourge of war. Its visitations had been in the first instance provoked by the turbulent partisanship of Frederick Ulric's brother, Christian, the Protestant administrator of the See of Halberstadt, and the devoted champion of Elizabeth of Bohemia. To Englishmen she must always be, as she was to their ancestors, the heroine of the Great War. The quick impulse of a high spirit, followed by the long devotion of an unflinching fidelity, identified the princess to whom the Hanoverian line was to owe its place in the English succession with the cause to which our nation's sympathies were given.

The Middle House of Brunswick, which, from the ordinary place of residence of its Dukes, had come to be called the House of Brunswick-Wolfenbüttel, had, with the subsequent sanction of the Emperor Charles V and the Estates of the Duchy, set up as the law of its territories the principles of indivisibility and primogeniture. The so-called *Pactum Henrico-Wilhelminum*, of 1535 [1], brought about by no very conscientious means, formed a precedent of considerable importance for the history of the House of Guelph. A precedent rather than a law,—since the line for the regulation of whose succession the agreement was devised, died out within a century; and in 1634, before the fury of the Great War had been spent, its dominions passed in different portions to the descendants of Henry, the elder of

[1] Cf. O. von Heinemann, *Geschichte von Braunschweig und Hannover*, vol. i. (Gotha, 1892), p. 336.

the two sons of Ernest, the last Duke of the Middle House of
Lüneburg. From them sprang the Dukes of Brunswick
of the Wolfenbüttel and Bevern lines, which, though not
participating in the Personal Union, were to be so closely
associated with some of the most momentous European conflicts in which Great Britain and Hanover were together
involved[1]. Duke Ernest's younger son, William, on the
other hand, was the actual founder of the New House of
Lüneburg, that was destined to inherit the British throne.
The politic design of uniting under a single rule the whole of
the dominions of the House of Guelph had been frustrated
in 1569 by the marriage of the elder brother, Henry, under
circumstances more or less analogous to those of the much-
vexed marriage between the parents of Sophia Dorothea,
afterwards unhappily wedded to the future King George I[2].
The dynastic principle, whose workings may be traced into
the later period of the Personal Union, could henceforth only
exert itself within the limits of each branch of the historic
House respectively. In the Lüneburg branch, possessed of
the Lüneburg-Celle territories, to which it added certain
minor acquisitions, and from 1635 the principality of
Calenberg-Göttingen, indivisibility of territory and unity
of government were established *in perpetuum* by the compact
of 1592, formally confirmed at Celle in 1610. In accordance with this agreement, the elder four of the seven sons of
Duke William held sway in turn at Celle, fortune so arranging
it that each of them actually succeeded on the death of his
next elder brother. But the very purpose of unification,

[1] Through Prince Ferdinand, the victor of Minden, Duke Charles
William Ferdinand, who fell at Auerstädt, and Duke Frederick William,
who fell at Quatrebras.
[2] Viz. Duke Henry married, in contravention of a previous agreement
with his brother that neither should take this step without the approval
of the composite authority under which the country had been previously
governed; and he now demanded a partition.

C

which has commended the compact to subsequent generations, caused it at the time to be vehemently resisted by the
Estates both of Lüneberg and of Calenberg. The latter in
fact exhibited the very spirit which many generations later—
in 1794—found expression in a resolution of the same Diet,
requesting the then Elector—King George III—to announce
to the French Republic the neutrality of the ' Calenberg
nation' in the Coalition War. Thus, the fifth surviving son,
the celebrated Duke George of Lüneburg, who in the Thirty
Years' War played a part both important and patriotic, for
a time held separate sway in Calenberg, of which he constituted the town of Hanover the capital ; and in his last
will he renewed the assurance to the Estates of the principality, that it should never be united with Lüneburg-Celle,
although, in accordance with the rule of primogeniture,
his eldest surviving son was to have his choice between
the two.

Had Duke George lived seven years longer, he might, by
his statesmanship, and more especially by the strength of his
position as a military commander, have secured to the House
of Guelph a prosperous issue out of the great war. As it
was, in the year after his death (1642), the Brunswick-
Lüneburg Dukes prematurely concluded a separate pacification at Goslar with the Emperor, and hereupon disarmed.
The consequences of this precipitation showed themselves
six years later in the Peace of Westphalia, when Hildesheim
had to be given up by Brunswick, while the Lüneburg Dukes
might count themselves fortunate in being excused from
meeting the exorbitant claims upon Calenberg of the heirs of
Tilly—a strange ancestor for a potential Hanoverian dynasty
—and in being allowed the modest ' satisfaction ' that at
every alternate election to the See of Osnabrück the Bishop
should be a prince of their family. You know how it was
a peculiar result of the Personal Union that the last Protestant

Bishop of the See, for whom it had been kept open more than two years, and who had been elected to it at the tender age of six months, afterwards became commander-in-chief of the British army, and was for a time thought likely to succeed to the British throne [1].

But to return for one moment to the latter half of the seventeenth century, the period when the fortunes of the Brunswick-Lüneburg line began to be built up in steady and unbroken progression,—greatly to the vexation of their kinsmen of Brunswick-Wolfenbüttel. To these jealousies, which afterwards led to certain notable attempts on the part of the elder line to ally itself by intermarriage with some of the chief reigning families of Europe, I cannot further refer ; they illustrate a witty saying of Elisabeth Charlotte, Princess Palatine and Duchess of Orleans—known I trust to some of my hearers as one of the most amusing letter-writers and one of the most brave-hearted women of her own or any other age. 'The history of the House of Brunswick,' she says, 'is just like the birthright of Esau and Jacob ; the elder brother lets his blessing be taken by the younger, and then wants to have it back again.' For some time, however, after the Peace of Westphalia, a consciousness of their common needs kept the Guelph governments on good terms with one another. Together they broke the obstinate resistance long maintained against the ducal authority by the city of Brunswick, where their nominal *condominium* was henceforth exchanged for the sway of the elder line [2]. Together

---

[1] A picture of the Duke of York in childhood, with mitre and crosier indicated in a corner of the canvas, used to be shown in the palace at Osnabrück.

[2] A *condominium* continued to exist elsewhere, notably in a portion of the Harz mountains, thence called *Communion-Harz* ; where this anomaly survived even the war of 1866, and was not put an end to till 1875. See Braun-Wiesbaden, *Bilder aus der deutschen Kleinstaaterei* (Hanover, 1881), vol. iv. pp. 259 seqq.

they revived the activity of the joint University of Helmstädt, whose greatest light, Calixtus, had shone almost solitary among the ruins of a noble seat of learning. Together, above all, they strove to vindicate to their House and to the Lower-Saxon Circle of the Empire an authoritative voice in maintaining the Peace upon which its security and cohesion depended. Thus in this period the loyal co-operation of the elder line added strength and significance to the foreign policy of the younger, some aspects of which have a very direct bearing upon our theme.

The dominions of the Brunswick-Lüneburg family were distributed among the sons of Duke George, on the twofold principle of maintaining the right of primogeniture, and that of indivisibility of territory except in so far as Calenberg (Hanover) was to remain separated from the more important Lüneburg-Celle. The Hanoverian historian Spittler—an author of notable lucidity of statement as well as solidity of research—makes a remark of which the bearings upon the later experiences of the dynasty will not escape you. When on the accession of the House of Hanover to the thrones of these islands Englishmen had set down that House and all its belongings as 'German,' everything seemed to have been said ; in truth, however, the type which the dynasty represented was in many respects a novel one in Germany itself. Spittler points out [1] that none of Duke George's four sons had in the old way gone through a University training, but that foreign travel, and more especially long-protracted sojourns in Italy, and at Venice in particular, had made the Lüneburg Duke, who for forty years stood at the head of the family, a prince on a new model, strongly contrasting with that followed by the Brunswick Dukes. This was George William, the close

---

[1] *Geschichte des Fürstenthums Hannover, &c.* (Göttingen, 1786), vol. ii. p. 181.

friend of our William III, who held sway at Celle from 1665
to his death in 1705, having in 1689 added to his patrimony
(by a much disputed inheritance) the duchy of Saxe-Lauen-
burg.   And the same remark applies to the fourth brother,
Ernest Augustus, the actual progenitor of our Hanoverian
kings.   These two princes were thus closely bound together,
not only by an affection that withstood the severest of trials,
but by a complete congeniality of disposition, habits and
opinions.   They thought and felt alike in both public and
private concerns, and alike united to an unflinching firmness
in the maintenance of the political interests of their dynasty
a moral laxity which was not less surely inherited by their
earlier descendants.   The third brother, John Frederick,
who held Calenberg (Hanover) from 1665 to his death in
1679, though equally fond with his brothers of Italian travel
and of French society, had in him more eccentric elements
of obstinacy.   In Italy he became a convert to the Church
of Rome ; and he was led into devious paths of policy partly
in consequence of this step, partly by a restless ambition
which at different times dangled before his eyes the Grand-
Mastership of the Germanic Order, and the Polish Crown [1].
On his death in 1679 Calenberg (Hanover) passed to the
youngest of the four brothers, Ernest Augustus, who since
1662 had held the bishopric of Osnabrück, and who in 1658
had married the Princess Palatine Sophia, the youngest
daughter of Elisabeth Queen of Bohemia, and the mother of
our kings to be.   Before the conclusion of this marriage
Duke George William, as heir-presumptive to Celle, had
entered into an undertaking not to marry (he had formerly
himself been engaged to the Princess Sophia) ; so that the

---

[1] See A. Köcher, *Geschichte von Hannover und Braunschweig*, vol. ii
(Hanover, 1895), p. 80.—Leibniz, who was admitted into the Hanoverian service by John Frederick, celebrated his virtues both in German
prose (of the ' Chancery ' sort) and in Latin hexameters.

ultimate succession of Ernest Augustus or his issue to Celle
seemed assured.   And even on the marriage in 1675, in
spite of this undertaking, of George William to a French
lady, Eleonora d'Olbreuse, hitherto his mistress, the rights
of their issue to the succession had been expressly barred
during the survival of any descendant of George William's
younger brother.   The sole impediment in the way of a permanent union of the entire dominions of the House of
Brunswicke-Lüneburg therefore now lay in the testament
of Duke George, establishing the separation of Calenberg
(Hanover) from Lüneburg-Celle.   This was met in 1682 by
the 'setting-up' (i. e. publication by anticipation) of the
testament of Duke Ernest Augustus, which in the following
year received the imperial sanction[1].   It proclaimed as
a perpetual law and *statutum familiae*, to be observed by all
the testator's descendants, the twofold principle of indivisibility of the existing territories of the House, including
Calenberg (Hanover), and of succession by primogeniture.
We may note as curious that shortly before the foundation
was thus laid of the future dynastic greatness of the House of
Hanover—for without the eventful union of territories just
indicated there could have been no question of a Brunswick-
Lüneburg electorate—the first step, though as it proved
a false one, had been taken towards the consummation of
that greatness by the acquisition of the British Crown.   In
December, 1680, Prince George Lewis (afterwards King
George I) visited England with a view to asking the hand of
the Princess Anne (afterwards Queen); but the project,
which was approved by her brother-in-law the Prince of
Orange, fell through, it was said—though we need not
examine the statement—because Prince George was not

[1] So Havemann, *Geschichte der Lande Braunschweig und Lüneburg*
(Gottingen, 1853), vol. iii. p. 295; see, however, Spittler, vol. ii.
p. 321.

attracted[1]. Two years later—but this time against the
advice of William of Orange—the Hereditary Prince George
Lewis was, in order so to speak to make assurance doubly
sure, married to Sophia Dorothea, the daughter of his uncle
Duke George William and his French wife, at last Duchess
of Celle. Into the tragic catastrophe of this marriage, which
casts a deep shadow over the history of the House of Brunswick in the beginnings of its period of greatness, it is unnecessary on the present occasion to enter. No estrangement
whatever was caused between Duke Ernest Augustus and
his elder brother by the divorce declared between the Hereditary Prince and Princess, or by her melancholy doom.
Less widely known is another cruel chapter in the history of
the dynasty, the origin of which is directly traceable to the
establishment of the combined laws of primogeniture and
indivisibility. These laws were bitterly resented by the
second son—Frederick Augustus—the 'poor Gussy' of his
mother the Duchess Sophia's candid *Memoirs*; and his
grievance was supported by a protest from the active pen of
his ambitious kinsman Antony Ulric of Brunswick-Wolfenbüttel. Prince Frederick Augustus afterwards lost his life
in the Turkish wars, in which he served like four of his
brothers, and in which one of them had previously fallen;
whereupon the next eldest survivors, the Princes Maximilian
William and Christian, refused to recognise the new statute.
With the countenance of Antony Ulric, and apparently also
with that of the celebrated Brandenburg minister Dankel-
mann, Prince Maximilian hatched a plot as to which information was forwarded to Hanover from Berlin by his sister,
the Brandenburg Electress Sophia Charlotte. At the end of
1691 he was arrested, together with the chief accomplices
of his schemes; but as in the case of the youthful escapade

[1] *Briefe der Herzogin Elisabeth Charlotte, &c., u. s.,* vol. i. p. 36;
cf. Bodemann, *J. H. von Ilten,* p. 10 and note.

of the future Frederick the Great, his own life was spared [1], while the most prominent of his agents, Colonel von Moltke, a high official of his father's court, suffered death as guilty of high treason.

The unity of the dominions of the House of Hanover (as, following later usage, I may henceforth conveniently call it) was now assured. But the fulfilment of this indispensable preliminary condition of its rise to high political importance would not have sufficed, had its bearing and action with regard to the affairs both of the Empire and of Europe at large proved inadequate to the demands made upon it. So far as their results have as yet been given to the world, the researches of Professor A. Köcher, the eminent historian of Hanover and Brunswick during the years (1648–1714) which we have at present in view [2], show that the part played by the princes of the House of Brunswick, and by those of the younger or Hanoverian line in particular, in the imperial and general politics of this period, was one of considerable importance, although little account was afterwards taken of this in England. During the earlier of these years their endeavours were chiefly, nor without success, directed towards preventing Sweden and France from breaking through the limits assigned to them by the Peace of Westphalia; and these are the very Powers with which we shall find the foreign policy of the House of Hanover still principally concerned at the time of its accession to the British throne. The Triple Alliance of 1668, however, in some measure shifted the relations between the leading European States. The Brunswick dukes were plied with solicitations on both sides, and, having already had experience of the guilders of the Dutch, they were now for

[1] He afterwards commanded the first line of cavalry at Blenheim, and died—as a Roman Catholic—in 1726.
[2] See especially. *u. s.*, vol. ii. pp. 79 seqq.

the first time in their history offered subsidies by the government of England [1]. We know how defective were the foundations on which the Triple Alliance rested, and how soon,
notwithstanding the importance for the peace of Europe of
the principle of intervention which that Alliance embodied, its
value as an effective instrument passed away. In 1671 John
Frederick of Hanover actually concluded a treaty of neutrality with France, which amounted to little short of an
alliance with the unbaffled aggressor; and George William
of Celle and Ernest Augustus of Osnabrück seemed not
indisposed to follow suit. It was in the same year that, with
the aid of the veteran diplomatist Gourville, whose *Memoirs*
describe his visits to the half-Gallicised courts of these princes,
Lewis XIV was persuaded to gratify the Duke of Celle by
a royal ordinance, naturalising his daughter in France as
'Demoiselle Sophie Dorothée de Brunswick et de Lunebourg [2].'
But though his brother Ernest Augustus had actually entered
into a treaty on behalf of his bishopric, George William of
Celle continued to hold back, and by the advice of his Chancellor Schütz declined to range himself among the friends
and favourers of France at the epoch of her invasion of the
United Provinces in 1672. This may without hesitation be
described as a critical moment in the history of the House,
and one upon which its subsequent connexion with that of
Great Britain largely depended. Schütz, the minister who
completely emancipated the policy of his master from the
French influences surrounding him, thus exercised a notable
influence upon the House so long served by himself, and
after him by his son-in-law Bernstorff [3]. Thus not only

[1] See *ib.*, vol. ii. p. 89, as to Sir Gabriel Silvius' mission to the House
of Brunswick in the spring of 1669.

[2] *Ib.*, vol. ii. p. 199.—I have only read Gourville's *Memoirs* in
Petitot's series, but a new edition has just been announced.

[3] The real name of the family, which served the House of Brunswick-

were George William of Celle, and with him his brother
Ernest Augustus, gradually gained over to the political
system of William of Orange and his mentor Count George
Frederick of Waldeck ; but the foundations were laid of
a policy which during some fourscore years, both before
and after the accession of the House to the British throne, a
series of trusted advisers, from Schütz to Bernstorff, and from
Bernstorff to Münchhausen, consistently strove to maintain.

The cardinal principle of this policy, that of a loyal
adhesion to the House of Austria, found expression in the
treaty concluded in April, 1674, between the Emperor
Leopold I and all the Dukes of both the Brunswick-Lüneburg and the Brunswick-Wolfenbüttel lines, John Frederick
of Hanover alone adhering to France till very shortly before
his death in 1679. By this treaty the Dukes, in return for
subsidies from the States General of the United Provinces,
Spain and the Emperor, undertook to furnish 15,000 men,
besides a further 2,000 at their own cost. There can be
no doubt that a strong national feeling, such as was less
rare in the seventeenth century than is sometimes supposed,
prevailed at this time in the Empire. Considerable enthusiasm greeted the successes against the French in 1674,
of which a full share fell to the Brunswick-Lüneburgers,
headed by their Dukes. These troops gained a brilliant
victory under Ernest Augustus and his son George Lewis
at the Bridge of Conz, and took part in the recovery of
Treves. But the advantage was not pushed, and the Dukes
returned home to protect their own territories against the
other arch-foe of the Empire, the Swedes, of whom soon

Lüneburg in at least three successive generations, was Sinold. The two
sons of Chancellor Schütz were in turn ministers at the Court of
William III, and his grandson was the unlucky Hanoverian minister at
the Court of Queen Anne who was sent away for having demanded
the writ for the Electoral Prince.

afterwards (in January, 1675) the great Elector of Brandenburg disposed at Fehrbellin.

After the Peace of Nymwegen Lewis XIV entered upon his
process of reunions, dissimulating the reliance placed by him
upon the Turk, who was more seriously than ever threaten-
ing the Empire from the East. The bonds of alliance were
hereupon drawn still closer between the imperilled House
of Austria and the Brunswick-Lüneburg Dukes, of whom
Ernest Augustus now held sway at Hanover in the place
of his deceased brother, the Catholic John Frederick. Of
the glories of the great day that saved Vienna from the
Infidel (September 12, 1683), not the least conspicuous
were earned by Prince George Lewis and the Hanoverian
life-guards[1]. From this time forward, as should surely be
remembered to its honour, the House of Hanover displayed
the keenest interest in the war against the Turk carried on
by the Emperor and his allies of the Holy League ; in 1685
a Celle-Hanoverian contingent, led by Prince George Lewis,
swelled the army of the Danube, and took part in the
capture of Neuhäusel. I have already mentioned the services of his brothers in the cause. Three of them took part
in the same campaigns, in which two of them lost their
lives ; and a fourth led out the first detachment of the
Hanoverian troops in the pay of the Venetian Republic, who
did not return home till 1688, after expelling the Turks from
Peloponnesus, and from the ruined Acropolis of Athens[2].
We shall see a little later that the Government of George I
was the first British Government of modern times that
directly intervened in a diplomatic way in Turkish affairs[3].

[1] See O. Klopp, *Der Fall des Hauses Stuart*, vol. ii. p. 400, and
Appendix xii.

[2] Bodemann, *Ilten*, p. 20.—I am sorry to say that it was a Lüneburg
officer of artillery whose bomb exploded the Parthenon (Zinkeisen.
Geschichte des osmanischen Reiches, vol. v. p. 134. note).

[3] See below as to the Peace of Passarowitz.—An odd relic of George I's

When, in 1688, no doubt partly in consequence of the successes of the Imperial arms in the East, the French irruption into the Empire took place in the West, Celle and Hanover joined in the Magdeburg Conference (October), and contributed 8,000 men to the force which occupied Frankfort and secured the Middle Rhine[1].   Duke Ernest Augustus, whose activity at this time is very noteworthy, commanded this force, with his eldest son George Lewis by his side, and was prominently concerned in the operations which in the following year led to the recapture of Mainz[2].

These services, rendered at the critical season when the Turkish war had not yet closed, and when the Grand Alliance was only on the eve of conclusion, merited a re-ward which was not wont to flow very copiously, viz. the 'gratitude of the House of Austria.' They were not the less welcome to the Emperor Leopold, as supplying a balance to the growing power and importance of Branden-burg, between whose political designs and action and those of the House of Hanover a peculiar relation henceforth becomes manifest, on which we shall have to dwell at length in certain of its later phases.   In the times immediately under notice this relation was made up of periodical co-operation and a growing jealousy; nor was it by any means dominated by the intermarriage between the two Houses in the persons of the Electoral Prince Frederick (afterwards the first Prussian king) and Sophia Charlotte, Ernest Augustus and Sophia's accomplished and amiable daughter (1684).

Hungarian campaign long survived in the two Turks captured by him as boys at this time—Mahomet (the ' honest Mahomet ' of Pope's *Moral Essays*) and Mustapha.   The report that as pages of the backstairs they exercised influence in political as well as in private affairs appears to rest on the authority of the Count de Broglie.   (See Jesse, *Memoirs of the Court of London from the Revolution of* 1688, vol. ii. p. 297.)

[1] Klopp, vol. iii. p. 198.
[2] *Ib.* vol. iv. p. 33 ; Havemann, vol. iii. p. 217.

This anxious jealousy of the advance of its Brandenburg neighbour both in actual power and in dignity of rank contributed to rivet the attention of the House of Hanover upon the establishment and improvement of its own position in the Empire. The cohesion of the dynasty had been ensured by the near prospect of a unification of its dominions, while its military strength had been raised by a continuous system of subsidy treaties with the Great Powers of the Grand Alliance. Nor was the attention of Ernest Augustus and his eldest son diverted from its main object by any anxious consideration of the possible advantages to be derived by their House from the English Revolution, and from the clause in the Bill of Rights excluding Papists from the throne. In the debates of the House of Commons it had been urged as one of the reasons for omitting in the Bill to name the House of Hanover in connexion with the succession, that any such mention would offer to foreign princes an opportunity for interfering in the affairs of the nation; and the proposal made by the House of Lords in conformity with the wishes of King William, to settle the reversion of the Crown upon the Electress Sophia and her posterity, had been rejected accordingly[1]. The interests of her husband and eldest son during the ensuing period were concentrated upon the question of securing the electoral dignity to their House. Early in 1692 was concluded the so-called Electoral Compact (*Kurtractat*), by which the two Brunswick-Lüneburg Dukes undertook to furnish, in addition to a money contribution, a body of 6,000 troops at their own cost for the prosecution of the war against the Turks, and after it of the war against France; while a supplementary agreement engaged both sides to perpetual friendship and military assistance in the

[1] Hallam, *Constitutional History of England,* ch. xv ; cf. Traill, *William III,* p. 72.

event of danger of war, and specially assured to the House
of Austria the support of Brunswick-Lüneburg in coming
Imperial elections and with regard to the imminent question
of the Spanish Succession. In return the Emperor promised to invest Ernest Augustus with a Ninth Electorate,
and in the December following the Investiture was actually
accorded. The bond which tied the House of Hanover to
that of Austria was therefore in both origin and conditions
altogether exceptional; and this should not be overlooked
in commenting on the hold which it retained over the son
and the grandson of Ernest Augustus. But though the
Investiture had been secured, the second and final part of
the procedure, viz. the admission of the new Elector into the
Electoral College at the Diet, took sixteen further weary years
to bring to pass. Before the expiration of this period (in
1708) the death of the Duke of Celle (in 1705) had at last
united the entire Brunswick-Lüneburg inheritance in George
Lewis's hands. The jealous intrigues of Antony Ulric of
Wolfenbüttel, the vacillations of Saxony, whose claims on the
Lauenburg inheritance were bought off, while the Elector's
enquiries concerning the terrible Königsmarck scandal were
met by an impenetrable silence, and a host of other obstacles,
were at last overcome by the ability and persistence of the
Hanoverian diplomacy [1]. Before success at last rewarded
its efforts, the ambition of the Elector of Saxony and that
of the Elector of Brandenburg (with whom Hanover had
concluded a *foedus perpetuum* in 1700) had alike been
satisfied, in 1697 and in 1701 respectively, by the coveted
acquisition of a royal crown.

Ernest Augustus had not survived to witness the com-
pletion of the most anxious and difficult task of his life. He

---

[1] The chief credit of these negotiations belongs to Jobst Hermann
von Ilten, the biographical account of whom by Dr. E. Bodemann has
already been cited. See especially pp. 26 seqq.

had died in 1698, leaving to his successor, together with the
prospect of a speedy and full recognition by his fellow Electors
of the dignity conferred upon his House, the assurance of a
solid and indivisible dominion, extended beyond the Elbe by
his own efforts, an exchequer free from debt, an effectively
centralised civil administration, and an army of some strength
and of high repute. He further bequeathed the tradition,
embodied in the form of a solemn compact, enjoining upon
his heir a firm support of the House of Austria, a loyal maintenance of the integrity of the Empire, and a steady resistance
against the aggressions of France, with whom peace had
been concluded at Ryswick in the year before his death.
Finally, he had contrived to remain on good terms with
Brandenburg, notwithstanding that, by no means to the dis-
satisfaction of his chief counsellors, this State had, in consequence of its geographical position, of the political genius of
the Great Elector, and of the perversity of the Saxon Court,
already become the foremost Protestant Power in the Empire.

In conclusion, a word must suffice to remind you how
during the sixteen years of his electoral rule before his
advent to the British throne George Lewis consistently
adhered to the principles of the paternal policy. With
Brandenburg he concluded in 1700, as was just now noted,
a perpetual alliance, after having in the previous year skil-
fully averted a conflict on the occasion of an encroachment
upon Holstein-Gottorp on the part of Denmark. His conduct
in face of the imminent renewal of the struggle with France
was prompt and spirited. In 1701 he and his uncle at Celle
joined the Grand Alliance re-knit by William III towards the
troubled close of his career; and in the following year they
forced their Wolfenbüttel kinsman to renounce his separate
alliance with France. When the great War of the Spanish
Succession broke out, Hanover and Celle placed more than
10,000 men under Marlborough's command-in-chief; nor

was it the fault of the Elector George Lewis that during the years (1707–10) in which he stood at the head of the Imperial forces on the Upper Rhine, he accomplished no military results of importance. His loyalty towards the cause of the Grand Alliance remained unimpaired, when, disappointed and vexed by the condition of the composite force under his command, he laid it down without having been able to gratify the military ambition which was probably the strongest personal impulse in him, as in his son after him. George I's northern policy, and his proceedings preliminary to the annexation of the Duchies of Bremen and Verden to his electoral dominions, will be more conveniently noticed in their connexion with the foreign affairs of his British reign. Due in the first instance to the action of Denmark, and to her manifest wish to anticipate him, the intervention of Hanover against Sweden was at all events consistent with the previous vigilance of his House against the inroads of a Power at whose hands the Guelph dominions had half a century before suffered so severely, and to the redistribution of whose conquests he could not pretend to remain indifferent. In the peace negotiations at Utrecht, which he could not but know must prove wholly unsatisfactory in their results for the Empire and its interests, the Elector George Lewis, although represented at the Congress, maintained an attitude of reserve [1].

And yet in the instrument of peace the rights of the House of Hanover to the British throne, now solidly established by the Succession Act in 1701, were asserted with a definiteness that left nothing to be desired. In this question of the Succession events had moved—not rapidly to be sure, but steadily—since King William III's visit to the Göhrde in the first year of George Lewis's electorship. On this occasion the King, had in reply to some leading questions suggested

[1] Klopp, vol. xiv. p. 454.

by the zeal of Leibniz to the enterprising Duchess Eleonora,
and put by her on her own responsibility, shown himself
favourably disposed towards the idea of the eventual succession
of the Hanoverian line [1]. At Hanover itself, the subsequent
endeavours of King William and the action of Parliament
were of course followed with interest; and after the formal
communication of this action, note was taken alike of the
unremitting efforts of the friends of the Protestant Succession,
and of the signals of fear proceeding from its adversaries,
sometimes ill-dissimulated under the guise of acquiescence,
or even of support. Gradually it became apparent that the
great body of intelligent public opinion in England was agreed
in favour of the legally settled solution of the question that in
the last years of Queen Anne occupied all minds. The ex-
pectations which neither the old Electress Sophia, nor those of
her descendants who in the course of nature would succeed to
her claims, could altogether refrain from indulging, variously
affected personal temperaments dissimilar to one another.
The Dowager Electress, although the intellectual centre of the
Court of Hanover, had never been consulted as to its policy,
still less admitted to the direction of its diplomatic action.
With all her wit and wisdom, she had largely to depend on the
guidance of her sentiments, into which she was far too high-
spirited, and far too true-hearted, not to allow both dynastic
ambition and inherited loyalty to enter. But, as you know,
she died a few weeks before Queen Anne, and the title of
Queen of Great Britain and Ireland was not inscribed on
her tomb. In her son, the Elector George Lewis, a rigid
reserve overlay a strong attachment not only to his Electorate but also to the system and usages of its government.
But he was cast in a mould of manhood, and when the hour
of action arrived his resolute will was rarely found unprepared for action. The personal ambition of the Electoral

[1] Klopp, vol. viii. p. 246.

D

Prince George Augustus, seconded by the aspirations of
his Princess, a woman of high intelligence and of rare judgment in conduct, awaited with comparative eagerness the
decisive tide in the affairs of the House. In order that it
might be taken at the flood, vigilant political agents of high
capacity and tried experience had for some time been busily
at work,—among them above all Baron Bothmer, the
Hanoverian resident in London, and at the Hague M. de
Robethon, the *alter ego* of the Hanoverian minister Bernstorff ; while the pens of publicists were equally on the alert,
including that of Leibniz, the faithful friend and correspondent of the old Electress, confident of the great destinies
and convinced of the great responsibilities of her House.

Whatever turn the course of events might take when that
House was at last called to the throne of a great nation,
which at no previous period of its history had attained to
such a height of power and influence in Europe, the first
Hanoverian King of Great Britain would still remain Elector
of Hanover, and would still be imbued with political traditions and principles of which it has been the object of the
preceding outline to recall some of the leading features.
Writing just before the passing of the Succession Act to her
beloved aunt the Electress Sophia, the Duchess of Orleans
had innocently assumed that when the throne of Great Britain
fell vacant her cousin George Lewis would become King of
Great Britain, while on the principle of the order established
by his ancestor his brother next to him in age would succeed
as Elector [1]. But, whatever consequences might thence
ensue for his old dominions or for his new, a Personal
Union between them had become an inevitable part of the
settlement brought about by the English Revolution, and
by the irrevocable downfall of the House of Stuart.

[1] *Briefe der Herzogin Elizabeth Charlotte, &c.,* vol. i, p. 485.

LECTURE II

THE SETTLEMENT

THE accession of George I would be very incorrectly described as the establishment of a petty German prince upon the British throne. Enough was, I hope, said in my first lecture to show that the part previously played by him as Elector, and after his uncle's death as ruler of the whole of the Brunswick-Lüneburg dominions, had been one of considerable importance for the Empire, and not without significance for the great political issues that occupied the attention of Western and Northern Europe. Quite apart from the interest reflected upon it by the question of the British Succession, and the many political transactions into which that question more or less materially entered, the House of Hanover, about the beginning of the eighteenth century, commanded a high estimation among the princely dynasties of the age. The dignified splendour of the Court of Hanover well responded to the consideration enjoyed by the Electoral Government; and although in many other contemporary capitals the example of Versailles had led to a new era of magnificence, yet we need not attribute solely to family partiality the assurance of the good Duchess of Orleans to the Electress Sophia (in 1705) that few sovereigns of the times lived in so much grandeur and dignity as her son [1].

[1] *Briefe, &c., u. s.,* vol. ii. p. 109. Cf. *ib.,* p. 331, as to the grand style in which *a.* 1713 George Lewis kept house at the Göhrde, entertaining 330 persons a day.

A sympathetic volume devoted by the worthy Master of the
Ceremonies of the late King Ernest Augustus of Hanover to
a description of the Court of his sovereign's ancestor and
namesake, goes some way towards proving his assertion that
this Court in no wise fell short of the contemporary standards
of Dresden and Vienna[1]. Under George Lewis, although
he personally hated ceremonial, both because it gives trouble
and because it is only rendered bearable by a graciousness of
which he cannot have believed himself possessed, the etiquette
of the Court increased in vigour very much in proportion as
its morality relaxed[2]. So long as the Electress Dowager
survived, there was fortunately no fear of intellectual interests
remaining wholly neglected at Hanover and Herrenhausen.
Thus, a shrewd English writer, who as the result of a visit to
Hanover in 1702 extolled its Court as 'extremely polite, and
accounted, even in Germany, as the best both for Civility and
Decorum,' dwelt particularly on the scientific and literary
atmosphere created by the Electress Sophia's exalted presence.
You are aware that King George I was not of a literary turn
of mind, although the correspondence remaining from his
earlier years indicates that he could express himself with
vivacity as well as sense; and I have already referred to the
familiar fact of his want of intellectual curiosity, as shown by
his not caring to learn the English language. His mother,
the old Electress, had spoken both English and Dutch to perfection, although it might be imprudent to accept without a
grain of salt the ecstasies of Toland, the author just cited, as

---

[1] C. E. von Malortie, *Der Hannover'sche Hof unter dem Kurfürsten
Ernst August und der Kurfürstin Sophie* (Hanover, 1847).

[2] See on this congenial topic E. Vehse, *Geschichte der Höfe des Hauses
Braunschweig*, vol. i. p. 163. It is here observed with truth that the
process noted above was analogous to that which occurred at Versailles
in the latter part of the reign of Lewis XIV, though of course the personal relations of the Grand Monarch to the ceremonial of his Court
were very different in character.

to her being 'entirely English in her Person, in her Behaviour, in her Humor, and in her Inclinations [1].' Sophia had been brought up abroad, and could consequently hardly be expected, in spite of herself, to resist this particular kind of flattery. King George I's refusal to take the first step towards earning a similar encomium, may safely be ascribed to an indifference to the thoughts and sentiments of others, thoroughly in keeping with his cold and selfish nature. Yet where either his preferences for persons or his own interests, as they presented themselves to him, were involved, he showed no fickleness of attachment or infirmity of purpose. From his public servants, whether as Elector or as King, he cannot be said to have ever lightly withdrawn his trust after it had once been given. According to the statement of a partisan of the Protestant Succession, the Huguenot whom after he had become a Whig writer Swift politely called a ' French dog,' some people fathered on King George I, others on his son and heir, 'the noble saying' that ''tis the Rule and Maxim of their Family, to reward their friends, do justice to their enemies, and fear none but God [2].' But though I doubt both conjectures as to the authorship of this apophthegm, it has in it a reminiscence of the truth. And, in order not to linger over personal estimates, it may be as well, in judging of the moral courage exhibited by George I when he made up his mind to face the certainty of an experience altogether repugnant to his natural inclinations, to go to the root of the matter at once. The nation of which on his own behalf and that of his dynasty he undertook the monarchical rule—

---

[1] See his *Account of the Courts of Prussia and Hanover*, printed in 1705. Toland, as Mr. Leslie Stephen says (*History of English Thought, &c.*, vol. i. p. 302), was partly dependent upon the patronage ' of foreign princesses of free-thinking tendencies.'

[2] See Abel Boyer, *The Political State of Great Britain*, vol. viii p. 326.

monarchical, whatever limits were imposed upon his authority
—was at the time by a *consensus* of foreign opinion judged
'wild to hold.'   During at least two generations it had been
generally regarded as impatient of permanent authority, and
as *a priori* disposed in particular to cast down any monarchical *régime* set up over it.   Undoubtedly there was more
of truth in this notion than would have been readily admitted
by that later generation of Englishmen from whose conservative sentiments the influences of the French Revolution seemed
on the whole to glance off so harmlessly.   Nor can there be
any doubt but that this impression as to the mutability of
English political feeling contributed, in conjunction with
a belief in the importance and tenacity of the Jacobite
remnant, to encourage the schemes of invasion entertained
by Alberoni and Charles XII [1].   As to the principal political
advisers and agents in whom George I trusted at the outset
of an experiment from his point of view both doubtful and unavoidable, a few hints may be of use before we advert to some
of the transactions of his reign in which their activity was conspicuous.   But in the first instance it seems necessary to take
note of the machinery which, from the establishment of the
Personal Union onwards, regulated the relations between
the royal and electoral governments, and as to which, unless
I am mistaken, some uncertainty has hitherto, in more respects
than one, prevailed.

The House of Hanover succeeded to the British throne by
Parliamentary title ; and the Act of Settlement (1701) con-

---

[1] So late as 1740 the Chevalier de Brosses, President of the Parliament
of Dijon, declared it impossible for the Old Pretender to renounce ' all
hopes of recovering the crown of a country so given to revolutions ' as
England, inasmuch as ' the spirit of the English nation is to hate the
ruling monarch be he who he may.'   See the quotation from de Brosses'
Lettres Familières (translated by Lord Ronald Gower), *ap.* J. E. C.
Bodley, *France* (1898), vol. i. p. 229.

ferring this title contained, as is well known, certain provisions introduced expressly with a view to an eventual
Personal Union between Great Britain and Hanover, together
with others directed generally to a restriction of the royal
prerogative.   With the latter we have no concern on the
present occasion ; nor need we, with regard either to these
or to the remaining provisions of the Act, pause to enquire
how far a retrospective as well as a prospective significance
attached to all or to any of them.   But as to the earlier clauses
of this famous instrument, set forth with so becoming an
amplitude by Hallam, a few observations will not be out of
place.

The throne, then, was to descend to the Electress Sophia
and her issue, *being Protestants.*   This condition accorded
with the primary purpose of the Act of Settlement itself, and
with the principle asserted in the Bill of Rights as an integral
and immutable part of the law of the realm.   In an age of
royal and princely conversions to the Church of Rome, neither
the House of Hanover nor the elder branch of the Brunswick
dukes was altogether exempt from the influence of this
tendency; under Duke John Frederick and his Duchess
Benedicta Henrietta, likewise a convert, Hanover was for
a series of years the centre of the Roman propaganda in
northern Germany and Denmark[1]; his brother Ernest
Augustus is said[2], but I do not know on what authority, to
have inclined in the same direction ; and his nephew Maximilian William actually followed his example at a later date.
A strong sensation was caused in 1710 by the public abjura-
tion of the Protestant faith by Duke Antony Ulric of
Brunswick-Wolfenbüttel, who three years earlier had induced

---

[1] Köcher, *u. s.*, vol. ii. pp. 53 seqq.

[2] By Father Theiner.   See his *Geschichte der Zurückkehr der
regierenden Häuser von Braunschweig und Sachsen in den Schooss der
Katholischen Kirche* (Einsiedeln, 1843), p. 6.

his niece Elisabeth Christina to take the same step in order
to obtain the hand of the Archduke Charles, titular King of
Spain and afterwards Emperor, and whose two daughters
within a few years followed their father into the Roman
fold. Even in the family of George I's mother Sophia,
whose parents had ventured and suffered so much for the
sake of militant Protestantism, one of her sisters—afterwards comfortably settled as Abbess of a French convent
—and one of her brothers had become Roman Catholics [1];
and her favourite niece Elisabeth Charlotte had changed the
creed which she professed, though not the sentiments and
opinions to which she remained staunch, when her hand was
given to the Duke of Orleans. But no such step needed to
be apprehended on the part of Sophia herself, fortified as
she was by an unswerving loyalty to the traditions of her
family, combined in her case with a courageous spirit of free
enquiry and a rooted dislike of theological controversy and
of its inevitable consequence, religious disunion. Nor was it
any more likely to commend itself to her eldest son, who was
little inclined to the recantation of opinions of any sort, and,
though it might not be easy to excite in him any interest in
the question of the union of the Protestant Churches, was far
from being preoccupied by a desire for any rigid formulation
of dogma. But the Act of Settlement, besides renewing the
general limitation of the Bill of Rights, had further provided
that whoever should hereafter come into possession of the
Crown should join in communion with the Church of England
as by law established. The Electress Sophia had through
life continued to profess the Calvinistic faith of the Palatinate
family; George I was a Lutheran like his ancestors. A few
months before his accession, Leibniz had demonstrated to
him the harmony between the Augsburg Confession and the

[1] Louisa Hollandina (afterwards Abbess of Manbuesson) and Edward.

Articles of the Church of England, and had found him both
well inclined to that Church, and incredulous of the preten-
sion that those who were zealous on its behalf were Jacobites [1];
and most certainly there was, as the event proved, no reason
for anticipating any difficulty on his part as to a sufficient
conformity. But the spirit of Leibniz and others who in this
age endeavoured to bring about a union between the Protestant Churches—intended by some, but not all, of its promoters
as a step towards a wider religious reunion—was not the spirit
prevailing among the English Churchmen, who in the year
of Queen Anne's decease, under Bolingbroke's unscrupulous
leadership, passed the Schism Act. The instructions drawn
up by Robethon for Baron Thomas von Grote, when sent to
London as the Elector's representative at the close of the
year 1712, were largely concerned—for the Electress Sophia
then stood first in the succession—with arguments meant to
convince the high-flying clergy of the Church of England that
the system of ecclesiastical government at Hanover was not
Presbyterian, but practically episcopal. But after the arrival
of King George I in England it was thought desirable to
print for circulation a specific *History of the Lutheran Church,
or the exact account of King George's Religion*, which provoked a reply with the telling title of *A letter of a schoolboy to
the author of the History of the Lutheran Church*. One of the
schoolboy's special points is the irreconcileable difference
between the Church of England and Lutheranism as to the
doctrine of the Real Presence. I know very well, continues
this innocent schoolboy, that King George was a Lutheran ;
but he is such no longer, being bound to defend our faith
against all erring sects and religions.

I cannot further pursue this subject, on which the late Pro-

---

[1] See *Correspondance de Leibniz avec l'Électrice Sophie*, ed. Klopp
(Hanover, 1874), vol. iii. p. 342 (*s. a.* 1711).

fessor Pauli published an interesting essay [1], from which I have
borrowed some of the above particulars. George I attended
divine service, and even communicated at the Chapel Royal,
St. James', although a Lutheran Chapel had been established
in connexion with the Court for the use of Queen Anne's
Danish consort ; while he granted divers favours to another
Lutheran place of worship in the Savoy, and was at least
solicited to show the same goodwill to a German Calvinistic
chapel likewise created there in the course of his reign [2].
For the rest, while towards the interests of Protestantism in
the empire George I proved himself so unmistakeably friendly
as, not long before his death, to be saluted in a British
Nonconformists' address as ' the common father of all Protestants [3],' his ecclesiastical policy at home was anything but
illiberal in spirit.   This was shown, *inter alia*, by his approval
of the endeavours of Stanhope in 1718 to abrogate the Test

[1] *Confessionelle Bedenken bei der Thronbesteigung des Hauses
Hannover in England*, in *Aufsätze zur Englischen Geschichte, Neue
Folge* (1883).

[2] See *Calendar of Treasury Papers*, 1720-8, ed. W. A. Shaw,
pp. ccxl. and 40. Curiously enough, in 1736, the bride of Frederick
Prince of Wales, Princess Augusta of Saxe-Gotha, who had of course
been brought up as a Lutheran, refused to communicate according to
the rite of the Church of England, and attended the administration of
the Sacrament in the Lutheran Chapel. However, on the representa-
tion of Sir Robert Walpole, Queen Caroline induced the Prince to
desire his wife to reconsider the matter ; or her later unpopularity
might have been in some measure anticipated. (See Lord Hervey's
Memoirs, vol. ii. p. 302).

[3] C. J. Abbey, *The English Church and its Bishops*, 1700-1800
(1887), vol. i. p. 204. It would obviously carry me too far were I to
dwell on this aspect of the foreign policy of George I, although it
should not by any means be overlooked. As a rallying cry 'the
Protestant cause' had considerable vitality left in it even after the Peace
of Utrecht ; and the very phrase may be met with as a sort of 'final
appeal' for both home and foreign use even in the despatches of
a diplomatist so cosmopolitan in his sympathies as Carteret.

and Corporation Acts, tempered though it was by a judicious
desire, into which Walpole fully entered, to avoid any appearance of antagonism to the interests, actual or supposed, of
the Church. His bearing in this respect altogether tallied
with the notable advice tendered to his dynasty, in a letter
among the Robethon Papers in the British Museum[1] from
Rapin de Thoyras, the French refugee who, after taking part
in the expedition of William III to these shores, wrote what
in its English dress served many of our ancestors in lieu of a
national history. Exhibiting, as was to be expected, a strong
feeling in favour of King George and the House of Hanover,
he expresses at the same time his conviction that the strength
of the Tories lies solely in their appropriation, so to speak, of
the cause of the Church of England. 'For this reason,' he
continues, 'I am persuaded that the single way of defeating
their manœuvres is to make it apparent that the Court has
no design of meddling with the Church, or of being guided
by the chiefs of the Presbyterian party.' I must abstain
from entering into any speculations as to the results of
the early Georgian *régime* upon the history of the Church
and of religion in England, whether in the direction of
a growth of tolerance among the better educated classes, or
in that of a stagnation of spiritual life under the operation
of the actual system of Church patronage. In this sphere
at all events, Queen Caroline's personal influence could not
even by herself be pretended to be a mere reflexion of
her consort's own profounder determinations. My wish is
simply to point out that the Personal Union gave rise to no
difficulty in the shape of a conflict with the provisions of the
Act of Settlement bearing upon the religion or religious
profession of the sovereign, although a party in the Church,
deficient neither in numbers nor in voice, would probably

[1] Vol. ix. pp. 127-130.

have been quite ready to make the most of such a conflict, had it been provoked by the dynasty [1].

Very different was the case with regard to the important clause of the Act of Settlement providing that in the event of the succession of a foreign-born sovereign the nation should not be engaged without the consent of Parliament in war for the defence of any dominions or territories not belonging to the Crown of England. This provision closely touches some of those transactions in the reigns of George I and II in particular, as to which it will be our business to enquire in more than one later lecture, whether or not, or in what degree, they were severally due to the Personal Union, and to its influence upon the foreign policy of Great Britain. But it may be as well at once to make the obvious remark, that the weakness of this clause lay in its ignoring a moral considera-tion from which no legal safeguard could dispense the parties, and more especially the stronger party, to such a political connexion. This obligation even so temperate a writer as Hallam, who regarded the Act of Settlement as having put the seal on our constitutional laws, held to have been unavoidable; or why should he, in his edition of 1827, pub-

---

[1] In any survey of the state of ecclesiastical policy after the accession of the House of Hanover, attention should be paid to Scotland, and to the influence of religious opinion traceable in the insurrections of 1715 and 1745 respectively. An interesting memorandum on the subject has been furnished to me by one of my hearers at Oxford, Mr. R. S. Rait, of New College, who will, I trust, sooner or later publish the result of his studies on this and cognate topics. He considers that Episcopalian Jacobitism practically disappeared from the Church of Scotland in 1716, and that from this date onwards the clergy of the establishment were devotedly loyal to George I and to George II after him. Outside the Church, the Episcopalians proper were almost without exception High Tories; but with them and the Roman Catholics were associated in opposition to the Hanoverian Government the Cameronians, who protested against 'the Prince of Hanover' as having been 'bred and brought up in the Luthren religion,' and also took part in the Jacobite risings.

lished only ten years before the dissolution of the Personal
Union, have placed on record his opinion that such a bond
ought never to have existed between the two States?   At the
same time, it is plain that the clause in the Act of Settlement
immediately under notice by no means aimed at impairing or
taking away the power of the Crown to make treaties, but
simply placed a sharp weapon in the hands of a Parliamentary
majority resolved on the impeachment of a minister held to
have given advice against the spirit of the Act.   For of course
there could hardly be a treaty—subsidy treaty or other—with
regard to which the applicability of the clause would not
admit of discussion.   Thus, in 1755, when an important
debate took place on the subsidy treaties concluded with
Hesse-Cassel and with Russia respectively, a member of the
House of Commons (Mr. Hume-Campbell) adverted to the
objections based on the Act of Settlement.   He said that he
should 'pay no compliment to it; it had been intended as
a censure on King William,' whose ministers had actually
been impeached in 1701 on account of the Partition Treaties;
'the clause specified was only declaratory, and did not take
away from the Crown the right of making treaties.   But
there had been subsidy treaties concluded, such, for instance,
as that with the Court of Wolfenbüttel in 1727, which it had
never been dreamt of impugning as contrary to the Act;
and in the present instance '—here was the gist of the matter
—'the treaties were calculated for the interests, and navy, and
commerce of Great Britain.'   Other and more important past
instances, to which reference will be made further on, were
cited; and when Pitt in his speech, while condemning the
treaties before the House, proceeded to review those of earlier
dates, he expressed astonishment at the supposed revelation
that 'Hanover was in them all[1].'   Whatever we may think

---

[1] See Horace Walpole (Lord Orford), *Memoirs of the Last Ten
Years of George II* (ed. 1846), vol. ii. p. 116.

of the motives and purposes of the particular treaties, the general issue raised in this debate sufficiently illustrates the fact that no real safeguard against the paramount danger of the Personal Union was erected by means of this much-discussed clause of the Act of Settlement.

The next clause, which prohibited any future sovereign from going out of the dominions of England, Scotland, and Ireland without consent of Parliament, had, as you know, an inglorious fate. It was repealed in 1715, previously to the first continental sojourn of King George I. After this he spent three further periods of some length at Hanover, and he had set out thither for a fifth time when his journey was stopped by death, and he was laid to rest in his beloved electoral capital. George II paid twelve visits to Hanover in the course of his reign,—spending thirty-four months there, it has been calculated, out of thirty-three years—during the last four of which the war perforce kept him in England. He was perfectly callous to the outcry on the subject, which rose to a higher pitch than it had ever reached in his father's reign, and which is one of the most familiar echoes that have come down to us from his own [1]. When his face was set towards Hanover and Herrenhausen, every other consideration became secondary. In 1745 he took his departure, amidst universal protests, on the very eve of an outbreak directed against the existence of his throne; in 1755 he turned his back upon a situation so serious that the safety of the realm itself seemed in jeopardy. On the other hand, George III

[1] In George I's reign, the King's absence had been lamented, and his speedy return more in sorrow than in anger desiderated, by the shop-keepers and artisans, who were convinced that business would flourish if he were in London. (See *Robethon Correspondence*, vol. viii. p. 267.) Under George II, these visits to Hanover became a political grievance, the cause of personal and social heart-burnings, and a constant handle for all sorts of satire.

never set foot in his Electorate during the whole of his reign,
and though he possessed some knowledge of the German
tongue, and had several of his sons partly brought up in
Hanover, as his father Frederick Prince of Wales had been,
he bequeathed very little of this knowledge to his successor
on the British throne. The attempt made after the recovery
of Hanover out of the hands of the French to delegate the
rule over it to a prince of the blood will be adverted to below ;
but this late development, which culminated in the Duke
of Cambridge exercising authority as viceroy, after he had
previously conducted the government without a title of
monarchical colouring, was obviously influenced by expecta-
tions of the coming separation.

The only remaining clause of the Act of Settlement which
calls for notice in the present connexion is that excluding
from the Privy Council, from Parliament, from any civil or
military office of trust, and from the benefit of any grant of
lands, all persons born of foreign parents out of the United
Kingdom or Ireland, whether or not such persons had been
naturalised. The exclusion from the Privy Council derived
additional significance from the circumstance, that another
clause of the Act sought to confine to this body the function
of advising the Crown on its measures of government. It is
known that this attempt to put an end to the Cabinet Council
system, which had prevailed under William and Mary, and
which for that matter continued to prevail under Anne,
proved a failure ; and that the Cabinet Council system
gained in importance by the fact that George I very soon
gave up the habit—not a very profitable one to a sovereign
unacquainted with the English tongue—of presiding at the
Cabinet Council meetings, although of course he continued
to attend those of the Privy Council. Henceforward Cabinet
Councils without the sovereign, which had formerly been
committee meetings only, became the rule. This arrange-

ment could hardly fail to lead to occasional misunderstandings, or to something worse, so long as the sovereign was in
the habit of consulting a *junta* of advisers who spoke his own
language.   For the avoidance of the disability imposed upon
foreigners in remembrance of William III's Irish land grants,
expedients were no doubt found in instances such as those
of the Duchess of Kendal and the Countess of Darlington.
Moreover, unlike the transfer of South Sea stock to the
Duchess, which required the royal sign manual, a very large
proportion of these ladies' gains must have remained secret[1].
But the exclusion of the Hanoverian subjects of our first two
Georges from official employment was consistently carried
out during the entire period of the Personal Union; in
return, no instances are on record of the admission of
British subjects into the Hanoverian service, except that
of Sir Hugh Halkett, who had been a distinguished officer of
the king's German Legion in the Peninsular War, and some
other similar permanent appointments to the Hanoverian
army of former legionaries after the peace of 1815.   Dr. von
Meier, who in his valuable *History of the Constitution and
Administrative System of Hanover* [2] notices this exception to
the mutual self-denying ordinance, contrasts the general
result with the relations between Denmark and the German
Duchies under the Personal Union between them which
came to so violent an end in 1866.   One used to hear bitter
complaints of the attempts to govern the Duchies from
Copenhagen; on the other hand, during many generations

---

[1] See Stanhope, *History of England, &c.* (5th ed.), vol. i. p. 213.
Concerning the South Sea stock, see *Calendar of Treasury Papers*,
1731-4, p. 237.

[2] Vol. i. p. 123.   Cf. *Dictionary of National Biography*, vol. xxiv.
p. 15.   Sir Hugh Halkett served in the Schleswig-Holstein War of
1848, commanding the 10th army-corps under Wrangel, and retired in
1858, when he was made a Hanoverian baron.

the higher posts of the Danish official world were largely filled by natives from the duchies, and with their aid German culture long helped to animate the social and intellectual life of the Danish capital. Nothing of the kind occurred in England. I have thought it worth while to go through the *Calendars of Treasury Books and Papers* for the years 1729–30, 1731–4, and 1735–9, very elaborately prepared by Mr. W. A. Shaw, as well as the earlier volumes covering the years 1720–8, in order to ascertain whether they exhibit any traces of appointments of Hanoverian subjects or other Germans to minor posts under George I or II, that might perhaps have been allowed to slip through the meshes of the Act of Settlement. But I have only come across a few German names belonging to doubtless deserving men nominated to tide-writerships, and to the holders of a court office or two [1]. I find in 1731 an (apparently) German auditor of the receipts for accounts relating to land-tax and malt-tax, and in 1728 the notice of the decease of one Thomas de Critz, sergeant-at-arms, but his office must have been held under one of the Houses of Parliament. More noticeable is the circumstance, that the diplomatic and consular service under the first two Hanoverian kings included a number of persons whom it is difficult to suppose to have been naturalised British subjects. Some of them may from their names be guessed to have been French refugees, or the descendants of such; others were Swiss; but one at least, a very active minor diplomatist. Charles Holzendorff, must have been of German parentage [2].

---

[1] This was held by Augustus Schütz under George II as late as 1737. The place of House and Wardrobe Keeper at Kensington Palace was likewise given to a German. Of course the Court was full of German domestics, and this practice, as every reader of Lord Hervey knows, continued under George II. He also mentions one Yager, 'German horse-apothecary at Hampton Court.'

[2] Holzendorff, whose name appears in the *Robethon Papers* in connexion with the Quadruple Alliance negotiations at Paris, became

Incidentally, it may be added that these *Calendars* mention no German recipient of any kind of pension charged to the public account, with the exception of this busy political agent, and of one other person in whose case the charge is on the Irish establishment[1].

But although the administrative systems of Great Britain and Hanover were thus, with a consistency that calls for respectful recognition, kept free from personal contact with one another, some arrangement had to be devised by which the Sovereign of both might in each be enabled to perform without inconvenience the functions of government incumbent upon him. Our first three Hanoverian Kings were, in their several ways, men of business in their attention to British affairs,—George I doing what was necessary, and George II and III doing a good deal more,—the former largely from habit of mind, and the latter in obedience to the notions that he had formed of his royal prerogative. Yet it

secretary of legation at Madrid under Colonel Stanhope (subsequently Lord Harrington), who was not strong in his knowledge of foreign tongues. (See *Robethon Papers*, vol. ix. p. 226.) The French and Swiss names in the diplomatic and consular service, with that of John Conraud, Under-Secretary of State, otherwise Secretary of the Latin Tongue (1735–6), are not really to the present purpose.

[1] These *Calendars*, I may add, contain no further statement of any significance as to the relations between the British and Hanoverian administrations in the period of the Personal Union. This may in part be explicable, as Mr. Shaw suggests, by the tradition (the correctness of which it is difficult to doubt) that Walpole destroyed all records of Secret Service expenditure under his control. By the way, one curious entry (*Calendar*, 1729–30, p. 8) refers to a proposed modification of our customs-tariff in favour of Hanover, by means of a diminution of 'the duty on linens, whether plain or those called Drell, manufactured in the King's German dominions.' I am not aware of any similar proposal in the way of commercial legislation till 1826, when the Second Chamber at Hanover resolved to take steps towards obtaining a relaxation of the British corn-duties in the case of Hanoverian corn; but the motion was rejected by the First Chamber, as certain to give offence to the King. (E. von Meier, vol. i. p. 142.)

would be quite a mistake to suppose that, all questions of
dynastic policy apart, they neglected the administrative business of their Electorate. Their interest in this ought to go
for something in the reckonings of the repeated sojourns in
Hanover of George I and II, that cost this country sums
hardly to be called extravagant, but neither to be set down as
altogether insignificant, both for 'rigging the convoys' for the
royal journeys, and for the expenses of the officials attending
on the King abroad[1]. George II's solicitude concerning
the internal affairs of his Electorate was, as will be seen,
otherwise attested; but they likewise engaged the attention
of George III, more especially when turning on agricultural
questions and the condition of the peasantry, or on trade
in general, or on the details of military administration [2].

Inasmuch, however, as from the first the sovereign of the
two countries was constrained to reside mainly in the more
important of the two, provision had to be made for the
ordinary transaction of business between the King and his
government at Hanover. And this was all the more necessary, since at the time of the accession of the House of
Hanover to the British throne the political system of the
Electorate had come to approach very nearly to an absolute
government exercised by the Prince himself or through his councillors. Of the functions appertaining to the estates of the several
duchies and principalities of which the Electoral dominions
were composed, a large proportion was exercised only by

[1] See *Calendars, ut s.*, 1720-8, pp. cclii and 72, and ccxlv and 53;
1729-30, pp. 68, 141, 257, as to charges for officials. Old Horace
Walpole's expenses, when entrusted with the duties of the Secretaryship
at Hanover in 1736, amounted to £3,000, in addition to £1,000 for
postage, stafets, &c. (*Calendar*, 1736-9, p. 259). The King's voyage
in 1729 cost £1,000 (*ib.* 1729-30, p. 273). There were of course 'mis-
cellaneous' charges, such as one for 'busts and pedestals' of King
George I transmitted to Hanover (*ib.* 1720-8, pp. ccl and 8); and
frequent charges for baggage, &c.

[2] E. von Meier, *u.s.*, vol. i. pp. 129-30.

means of standing committees; and while their legislative
duties were wholly insignificant, the financial extended merely
to those branches of expenditure and receipts of which the
estates possessed the control.   The conduct of the government was determined by an Ordinance (*Reglement*) promul-
gated by George I before he left Hanover for London in
1714, based to some extent upon a previous ordinance issued
by his father Ernest Augustus in 1680, but with modifications
to suit the regular conduct of the administration in the
absence of the Elector.   This Ordinance remained the basis
of the Hanoverian governmental system, and certain of its
provisions were reaffirmed in an edict concerning the reform
of the administration put forth in 1822 during the Governor-
Generalship of the Duke of Cambridge, and in the funda-
mental constitutional law (*Staatsgrundgesetz*) adopted in 1833,
during his viceroyalty.

The most important of the clauses in this Ordinance
referred to the delegation of authority by the Elector to the
Privy Councillors whom he left behind him at Hanover, and
whose sphere of action was necessarily enlarged from that
assigned to them by the father and immediate predecessor of
George I.   There was no lack of precedents in the way of
temporary enlargements of the same sort, for Ernest Augustus
and his brothers had been frequently absent from their
governments while detained by urgent private pleasures at
Venice or Rome.   In 1694 the number of the Privy Councillors (*Geheimräthe*) was five, but it seems to have been
slightly increased under George I.   These Privy Councillors
—or, speaking more accurately, their successors,—were the
dignitaries whom the impatience of Frederick II execrated as
the *perruques d'Hanovre*, and who collapsed before the
aggressions of Bonaparte.

Some obscurity seems to me to envelope the question,
whether in the earlier days of the Personal Union there was

a Prime Minister, properly so called, at Hanover. We know that there was no minister holding such a title officially in London; that the notion of a Prime Minister is foreign to the British constitution, and that it was consistently repudiated by the very statesman, Walpole, who was the first thoroughly to realise it in this country[1]. At Hanover there clearly always was, as in a State governed on strong monarchical principles there could hardly fail to be, one leading minister; but under George I, and probably also under George II, the title of President seems to have referred to the Elector's Chamber (I presume essentially a financial board) rather than to his Privy Council. The Prime Minister as such had no precedence over the other Privy Councillors, and within the Council the votes were equal, so that there was frequently a tie, the decision remaining with the King, or practically with the Hanoverian minister who, as we shall see, was in attendance on him in London. Matters were, of course, much simplified when, as in the days of the Münchhausens (under George II and III), the leading minister at Hanover and the minister in attendance were brothers, and acted in perfect understanding with one another[2].

[1] Although the nature of the office of Prime Minister has shaped itself distinctly enough in our later history, considerable uncertainty continues to attach to some of the functions supposed to appertain to it. Mr. Gladstone and Lord Beaconsfield are understood to have held different views as to the relations between the Prime Minister and his colleagues; the former, besides regarding himself as the sole organ through which the recommendations of the Cabinet should be communicated to the Sovereign, deeming it not incumbent upon him to make her acquainted with any differences of opinion in the Cabinet unless they should have reached the point of one or more resignations. Prince Bismarck's final retirement from public life was ostensibly caused by a conflict as to the relative responsibilities of a Prussian Prime Minister and his colleagues.

[2] See E. von Meier, vol. i. pp. 181–5.—The elder Münchhausen certainly seems to have been 'declared Prime Minister' by electoral rescript; but the evidence is not quite satisfactory. Cf. *Zeitschrift des histor. Vereins für Niedersachsen*, Jahrgang 1891, p. 153.

The most important division of business with which the Elector reserved to himself the right of dealing independently of his Privy Council was that concerned with military affairs —in so far as they came under the designation of *purè militaria*, and comprised such matters as the organisation and disposition of the armed forces of the Electorate, the appointment and dismissal of its officers, &c. For, although the army was in a large measure maintained by the votes of the Estates, the principle remained intact that the control of it was a matter entirely for the Elector. Thus he alone was responsible for, and if we like so to express it, profited by, the subsidy treaties into which as Elector he entered with himself as King of Great Britain, just as he or his father before him had concluded similar treaties with the Emperor, the States-General and the Signiory of Venice. And indeed it should be remembered that the troops of which the Elector thus disposed according to his own choice, were mercenaries, who had entered into a bargain with him for their services, rather than subjects called under arms by the law of the land. For although the system, besides being financially extravagant, must have involved much hardship and cruelty, and cannot therefore be looked back upon without regret, yet it was the inevitable result of the combination of the mercenary system with absolute rule. Indiscriminate charges as to the sale of human flesh and blood are unjust, not only to many of the princes concerned, who as commanders honourably shared the experiences of their comrades, but also to many a gallant officer or brave soldier in whose eyes warfare was the most eligible of professions or handicrafts [1].

---

[1] It would be well worth while for some well-informed writer to attempt a history of our subsidy treaties, from the time of its commencement to that of the American War of Independence. Our employment of German mercenaries in this gave rise to a resentment, without which it is doubtful whether the Colonies would in the last instance have desired separation. In its earlier stages such a history would have to include a

The Elector's direction of 'purely' military affairs was exercised on his behalf by the general commanding-in-chief at Hanover, who thus had practical control of everything connected with the command and discipline of the army,—while all matters bearing on the condition of the troops, their pay, arms, commissariate and the like, and to the very important business of recruiting, were managed by a board called the War Chancery, which like the Commander-in-Chief, reported direct to the King, with or without previous consultation with the Privy Council. To be sure, in cases of necessity the Privy Council was provided with special powers, and in the event of an actual imminence of war was authorised to conclude alliances, and in conjunction with the general in command to mobilise the troops. But how unsatisfactorily the conditions of the Personal Union caused so carefully adjusted a scheme of responsibility to work, we shall I hope find time to see in speaking of the most humiliating of the catastrophes which fate had in store for an army whose history notwithstanding remains full of honour—the capitulation of 1803.

In foreign affairs the Elector left current business to be carried on by the Privy Council or Ministry (for it had now practically become such) at Hanover. It may be thought creditable to George I's good sense, that the electoral residents at Ratisbon were bound to send their formal relations

good deal of correspondence of the nature of the letter addressed to Robethon by Dehn, minister of State at Brunswick, under date October 6. 1718 (*Robethon Correspondence*, vol. x. pp. 180–4). The writer represents that arrears of subsidies are still outstanding, and that a renewal of the subsidy treaty is still awaited, although his master has kept four regiments at the disposal of his Britannic Majesty, even under the highly rigorous condition of their being liable to be employed against any enemy whatsoever indicated by the King. A favourable response is claimed in consideration of the King's relationship to the Duke, and of the reflexion of glory falling from the royal house upon the *maison originaire*.

to the Ministry, and only brief summaries to the Elector ; the diplomatists accredited elsewhere had to transmit duplicate despatches to Hanover and to London.   In penal justice the Prince delegated to his Privy Council, as was in the nature of the case inevitable, the confirmation of sentences when requisite, but reserved to himself the exercise of the prerogative of mercy.   And, while this was only right and reasonable. he likewise kept to himself the right of appointments of all kinds ; for there is no species of authority which fails to cling to patronage as the most cherished of its privileges.   The appointments in question included those to the Privy Council or Ministry itself; for though it has frequently been represented as having been a co-optative body, no evidence exists of its having been so much as consulted in filling up vacancies upon it more than four times during the entire period of the Personal Union.

Inasmuch as in addition to any business falling under the above-mentioned heads, all serious expenditure had necessarily to be reported for the Elector's approval, a large amount of material had in the ordinary course of things to be sent on to London for the Elector's signature, or at least for his information.   At the close of every quarter the Privy Councillors despatched a courier with their statements of accounts, arranged under their respective heads of revenue and expenditure and settled by the Council, together with other papers ; and couriers were likewise sent on extraordinary occasions ; ordinarily the post sufficed, which probably travelled about as quick as the couriers,—or about as slow. All reports forwarded by the Council to London were addressed to the Sovereign in person, and all decisions thereon were returned in his name, and with his sign manual.   Thus a very large quantity of business continued to flow in for settlement by the King, much of it being of a kind which in comparison with the matters brought before him by his

British ministers was intrinsically insignificant. It has been estimated that at least half the time, devoted by our Hanoverian monarchs to the transaction of public business was —necessarily, so to speak—given up to that of the Electorate. This conclusion is of some moment; for there can be no doubt that such a distribution impaired the Sovereign's sense of proportion in giving his mind to British and Hanoverian interests respectively,—more especially in the case of King George II, who was not only intent upon governing, or at least seeming to govern, for himself [1], but was sincerely conscientious in his attention to the details of business.

Incidental reference has already been made to the practice, according to which one of the Privy Councillors—a member, in other words, of the Hanoverian Ministry—was in attendance upon the King, in order to lay before him and explain the material transmitted, to draft and put in form the royal decisions and replies, and to verify the accounts. In the performance of these functions he was assisted by confidential secretaries and clerks, and attended by an official messenger. These persons together constituted the so-called German Chancery in London, to whose activity a rather mysterious importance has occasionally been attached, but whose actual composition and duties have not hitherto, so far as I know, been made clear to English readers. Nor should I have been able to place the present information on the subject before you, but for the timely appearance of the first volume of Dr. von Meier's work already cited, and more especially for the great courtesy and kindness of Dr. Doebner, State Archivist and Councillor of the Archives at Hanover, in furnishing me with a complete and lucid statement on the subject, drawn up by one of the officials associated with him.

You will perhaps notice in passing that this Hanoverian

[1] See Lord Hervey's *Memoirs*, vol. i. pp. 93 and 186.

Chancery, familiarly, but not till a late date (1824) officially, known as the German Chancery in London, was not the earliest German establishment directly connected with the English official world to which that name has been given. The term Chancery, in the primitive sense which it retains in some other modern languages, of a secretarial office and repository of confidential documents, specially recalls to the historical student that period, full of diplomatic manœuvrings and the clandestine movements of secret agents, which preceded the outbreak of the Thirty Years' War. We think more especially of the Chancery of Anhalt, the agent-in-chief of the militant Calvinistic party of which the destined figure-head was the Elector Palatine, the husband of the English Princess from whom the House of Hanover derived its claim to the English throne. In the years following closely upon the overthrow of the Bohemian throne of Frederick and Elizabeth, and, as may be assumed, already in the interval of doubts and difficulties that had preceded it, there existed in London a German Chancery. This was obviously a secretarial *bureau*, set up to assist the Secretary of State in the conduct of German business, and primarily we must suppose to supply English translations of German documents, as well perhaps as German versions of communications addressed to Princes of the Empire and others by the Pacificator on the English throne [1].

Unlike the German Chancery of our first Stuart King, that of our Hanoverian Sovereigns was in no sense a branch of the English Foreign Office. Its local habitation was in St. James' Palace; for I notice among the *Treasury Papers*

---

[1] One of the persons employed in this earlier German Chancery was Rudolf Weckherlin, who afterwards, according to his own account, acted as Under-Secretary to four English Secretaries of State in succession; and who was moreover a poet of merit, and reproduced in his native tongue certain fine stanzas written by Sir Henry Wotton.

for the year 1726 [1] a letter to the Lords of the Treasury, for orders to be given 'for five wainscot presses for keeping the records of the German Chancery at St. James'.' These presses must in course of time have overflowed ; for the registers of the papers of the Chancery (the whole of which, so far as they remain in existence, are preserved in the State Archives at Hanover) cover the entire period of the Personal Union, from 1714 to 1837. All these papers were removed from London to their present resting-place on the accession of King Ernest Augustus; but two or three years afterwards —in 1839–40—their bulk was diminished by more than one-half. All those documents of which counterparts were to be found in the registers of the Hanoverian Ministry of State—formerly known as the Board of Privy Councillors— and which, as chiefly dealing with home affairs, possessed no historical interest, were at that date destroyed. Already, however, before the transportation of this large collection of State papers to Hanover certain other gaps had been made in it ; for on the occasion of the decease of each successive King-Elector the practice seems to have been regularly observed of destroying any personal letters from him to be found in the Chancery Archives [2].

In theory this Chancery was nothing more than a secre- tarial office for the service of the Elector during his 'tem- porary' absence from the Electorate—a travelling Chancery (*Reisekanzlei*). The Privy Councillor or minister in attend- ance upon the King in London, together with the secretary and clerks of the Chancery there, was regarded as absent from Hanover on special duty ; and his name was accord- ingly entered in the official calendar published at Hanover as

[1] *Calendar, &c.*, 1720-8, ed. J. Redington, pp. cccvii and 17.
[2] E. von Meier, vol. i. p. 125 ; where a letter is stated to have been exceptionally preserved, written on December 17, 1769, by King George III to G. A. von Münchhausen.

a member of the Privy Council, with the addition of the
words 'at present in London.' It was not till 1824, when,
as I have previously mentioned, the wish prevailed to make
the Hanoverian system of administration as complete in
itself as possible, that the German Chancery in London was
officially mentioned among the Hanoverian State authorities.
In practice, very much necessarily depended, both for the
government of the Electorate and for the continuous exercise
of a Hanoverian influence on the King, upon 'the Hanoverian Minister in London,' as he came to be usually
called [1]. When George I arrived in England in 1714, he
was accompanied by two Hanoverian ministers, Bernstorff
and Görtz, and he found a third there, Bothmer, who in his
post as Hanoverian envoy had done more than any man to
promote the Hanoverian Succession. But Bernstorff, as we
shall see, remained behind in Hanover after the King's visit
there in 1720, and altogether retired from office in 1723;
and Görtz returned early to Hanover as President of the
Financial Chamber (*Kammerpräsident*); while Bothmer's
position was quite exceptional, inasmuch while formally
a member of the Hanoverian Privy Council he continued to
hold the appointment of Hanoverian envoy—representing
the Elector at the Court of the King—till his death at
London in 1732 [2]. From an early date in the reign of
George I, the younger Hattorf, who had accompanied the
King to England in the place of his father, an old and valued

[1] The nearest analogy to the position of this minister with which
I have met is that of the Hungarian minister *a latere*, who is attached to
the Court of the Emperor-King, acting towards him as the representative
of the Hungarian Cabinet.

[2] I suspect it to have been in this capacity, that when Bothmer
remained behind in England during George I's visit to Hanover in
1716, he was in the habit of transmitting to the King more or less
elaborate *relations* of what occurred during the royal absence. Cf.
Kobethon Correspondence, vol. viii. pp. 319 and 325.

electoral official, performed the duties of minister in attendance, and countersigned the royal ordinances ; and on the accession of George II he was one of the batch of actual Hanoverian ministers named by the new Sovereign.   Henceforth, during the period of the Personal Union, it was the invariable custom to entrust the functions of minister in attendance to a single member of the Hanoverian Privy Council only ; and in the century following upon the death of Hattorf in 1737 a series of seven such ministers held office, including the younger Münchhausen (Philip Adolf) and Münster,—but the latter, in the Napoleonic period from necessity and after 1815 by preference, was rather a Prime Minister *in partibus* [1], than the representative of a body of colleagues.   Another eminent statesman, who as Prussian Chancellor of State was to acquire an enduring celebrity—Hardenberg—was in his younger days much chagrined by twice missing an appointment to the influential post of minister in attendance [2].   It should be added that the King-Electors at no time considered themselves prevented from consulting any other of their Hanoverian ministers by letter, or from sending for them in person ; moreover, the functions of the so-called London minister necessarily ceased during the residence of the King-Elector in Hanover, unless, as was largely the case in the times of George I, the minister accompanied the Sovereign across the water ; for in his Electorate he of course had at his command the service of all his electoral councillors.

In sum, the governmental system described above was probably as good a one as could have been devised to meet the circumstances of the Union, but proved incapable of averting its unsatisfactory results.   The resident ministry at

---

[1] This apt expression is used by Münster's biographer in *Allgemein- Deutsche Biographie*.

[2] The names of the confidential secretaries in the London Chancery have likewise been preserved.

Hanover never pretended to an authority in electoral affairs superseding that of the non-resident Elector, and was never less happy than when left by him to act for itself. Almost entirely composed of members of the old nobility of the land, it showed little or no desire to pass beyond its ordinary sphere of action; and at no time, so far as I am aware, identified itself corporately with schemes or ideas of policy outside that sphere. There is equally little reason for supposing that it ever allowed itself to be influenced by dishonourable or corrupt motives. In 1758, not long before his death, George II put forth a rescript calling upon his Hanoverian ministers to take into their consideration the boast of the French Government of the day that a large proportion of the Privy Council at Hanover had been ' at the disposal ' of France. This insinuation, savouring of traditions which in the earlier and later Stuart times even some English statesmen might not have found it easy to prove obsolete, was apparently not taken seriously at Hanover, and had probably only been communicated by the King-Elector in a spirit of superior irony [1]. Nor was the practice of attaching to the person of the King-Elector a Hanoverian minister charged with advising him in electoral affairs, in itself calculated to create or encourage in the Sovereign's mind a confusion between what may roughly be distinguished as his royal and his electoral policy. On the other hand, the large amount of Hanoverian business regularly received for transaction by the King, could hardly fail to demand an excessive share of his

[1] It may be worth noticing in this connexion that a M. de Bussy, clerk in the French Foreign Office, who was proposed as French diplomatic agent in Hanover during George II's visit there in 1755, had been in English pay when similarly employed by his government in London. Newcastle expressly enquired from Holdernesse, whether in the event of de Bussy's coming to Hanover this arrangement could be renewed. (See R. Waddington, *Le Renversement des Alliances, &c.,* p. 101.)

time and powers, while it was only too likely to distort his estimate of their due apportionment. Furthermore, it was quite inevitable that the Hanoverian minister in attendance on the King in London, who as such had the privilege of direct access to the royal presence, should, even apart from the special circumstances existing in the initial period of the Personal Union, command opportunities of an exceptional kind for exercising an inordinate influence upon the Sovereign's views and action, in regard to the affairs of Great Britain as well as to those of the Electorate. And of these opportunities exceptional advantage would of course be taken by a personage of unusual ability or address.

No doubt it was from the former point of view—that of the great pressure of business created by the double system —that George II, who bestowed a closer attention than his father before him upon the public business of both his kingdom and his Electorate, gave the most unmistakeable expression to his sense of the serious inconveniences involved in the Personal Union. At different times in his reign we find him recurring to the thought which already before his accession a different kind of motive had suggested to him, that a separation of the Hanoverian from the British sovereignty might be of advantage to both countries. The first notion of undoing the Personal Union seems to date from 1725, unless indeed we are to take into account the strange fancy which occurred to George I a few years earlier, before his reconciliation with his son, that the Prince might be compelled by Act of Parliament to undertake to resign his Hanoverian dominions on his accession to the British throne. This kind paternal design was abandoned in consequence of the adverse opinion of the Lord Chancellor Parker (afterwards Earl of Macclesfield), who had been formally consulted on the subject[1]. In 1725, two years before his own

---

[1] Coxe, *Life of Sir Robert Walpole* (ed. 1816), vol. ii. pp. 12-13. This

accession to the throne, the future King George II and his consort appear to have taken into their consideration, as a desirable family arrangement, a scheme by which their elder son Frederick should ultimately succeed in Hanover, and the younger William (afterwards Duke of Cumberland) in Great Britain. The feelings entertained towards Prince Frederick by his parents must be concluded to have thus early—when he was thirteen or fourteen years of age—settled in the direction in which they afterwards continued to flow; but King George I would not hear of the proposed arrangement being made unless Prince Frederick, who had hitherto been kept at Hanover, signified his assent to it, Walpole having warned him that unless he brought his grandson over to England the latter would never be allowed to set foot on English soil. The plan thus fell through; but in 1737 the idea of a separation was revived under different conditions. Frederick Prince of Wales was then in open opposition to his father's government; and it was with a view to annoying his elder son that the King mooted the plan of securing the succession to the Electorate to his younger brother. The Prince of Wales, so the rumour ran, would not have been unwilling to relinquish his claims to the Electorate in return for the doubling of his income (from £50,000 to £100,000 per annum). When Lord Hervey mentioned the proposal to Sir Robert Walpole, the latter cordially approved of it, and declared that if it were ever brought before Parliament it might be carried with universal concurrence of approbation.

idea seems to have been entertained as far back as 1700–1, when, as already mentioned, it was proposed to bring over the young Electoral Prince (afterwards King George II), so as to settle him in England and accustom him to English ways, while he should renounce his rights to the Succession in the Electorate. But at that time the British Succession had not come to be looked upon as so assured an expectation as to make it worth while to pursue the plan. (See Klopp, vol. viii. p. 556.)

His only fear was that if the scheme were carried, the King's interest in Hanover would be redoubled, and that while for the time every effort would be made to 'hoard' these for the Duke of Cumberland's grandeur and profit, and for the Queen's security and retreat, Hanover would be more of an obstacle and a source of difficulties than ever. Walpole actually conferred on the subject with the King and Queen; but the proposal was put aside at her instigation, Lord Hervey having moreover very sensibly pointed out that the consent of the Emperor and Empire would have to be obtained for the proposed arrangement, and that this could scarcely be expected, as the King of Great Britain must be so much more amenable to Imperial influence while he remained Elector of Hanover. King George II, however, according to Lord Hervey, continued to dwell on the scheme, and caused drafts and instruments to be prepared; but the matter was kept entirely private, and only guessed at even by Sir Robert Walpole[1]. In 1741, however—or at all events shortly before his downfall—the minister 'tantalised' Speaker Onslow, who is himself the authority for the anecdote, with the prospect of a message from the King to the House of Commons, in favour of the passing of an Act of Parliament, which should prohibit *in perpetuum* the joint inheritance and possession of Kingdom and Electorate[2]. Rather different from this project was another, of which (according to Horace Walpole) the Duke of Cumberland told Lord Waldegrave.

---

[1] Lord Hervey's *Memoirs*, vol. ii. pp. 216 seqq.

[2] See Coxe's *Life of Sir Robert Walpole* (ed. 1798), vol. ii. pp. 571–2. The Speaker replied that it would be 'a message from heaven'; but the message never came, and the Speaker was of opinion that had it come, it would have been rejected by Parliament as proceeding from Walpole. In any case, the opportunity was lost; and though the Prince of Wales was said at the time to have favoured the scheme, Speaker Onslow may have been right in his conjecture that King and Prince were alike too fond of Hanover to have been likely to regret its abandonment.

F

A so-called secundogeniture was to be set up for the Duke in the Hanoverian dominions themselves, to consist of the purchased principalities of Bremen and Verden; but the Duke remaining unmarried, the scheme was relinquished by his father. Had this martial prince been of a more susceptible disposition, the hazards incurred by the acquisition of these territories would not have been diminished; while the difficulties arising out of our connexion with Hanover in the Seven Years' and Napoleonic Wars might conceivably have been augmented.

Our earlier Hanoverian monarchs were not likely to feel very keenly the second of the objections suggested above,— viz. that founded on the exceptional opportunities for acquiring a personal influence over the Sovereign enjoyed by the Hanoverian minister in attendance upon him. To what extent advantage was actually taken of these opportunities is, however, precisely one of those problems connected with our subject on which but scanty light has been thrown by historical research. From the nature of the case, the period which in this respect more particularly comes into question must be the earlier portion of the history of the Personal Union; and it may therefore serve as an appropriate Appendix to my present lecture, if I add a short notice of the chief representatives and agents of Hanoverian statesmanship, by whom George I was surrounded at the time of his advent to the British throne.

APPENDIX TO LECTURE II

THE 'HANOVERIAN JUNTA' UNDER GEORGE I

NOTHING could be further from my wish than to attempt
a sketch of the Court of George I, and it is therefore unnecessary
to enter into a discussion of the channels through which whatever political influence was personally exercised upon the King
habitually reached him. Unless contemporary accounts are in-
correct[1]—which on this head there can be no reason for supposing
them to be—the personal *entourage* of King George I, from his
body-servants upwards, consisted, with the exception of Mahomet
and Mustapha, entirely of Germans. Even at his friendly
dinners on Richmond Hill with Sir Robert Walpole he was
surrounded by his German intimates ; and, in the genial words
of Sir Robert's son, ' it was not till the last year or two of his
reign that their foreign Sovereign paid the nation the compliment
of taking openly an English mistress [2].' For a long time he was
in the habit (following therein the example of both Charles II
and Lewis XIV) of transacting business of State in the apart-
ments of the Duchess of Kendal, who, notwithstanding the
contemptuous expressions of Sir Robert Walpole, can scarcely
have been altogether devoid of intellectual capacity, and who at
all events seems to have been credited with it by her brother,
the famous Marshal. But neither she nor the Countess of
Darlington, whose influence that of the Schulemburg gradually

---

[1] See, for instance, that of the Count de Broglie in 1721, cited by
Vehse, vol. i. p. 207.

[2] *Reminiscences of the Courts of George I and George II*, in vol. i. of
Letters (ed. Cunningham, 1888), p. cv.

eclipsed without quite superseding, and who showed some inclination for the society of wits and men of letters, appears at any time to have been lifted out of the region of personal intrigue into that of political designs. And in the great Court crisis of 1720, which ended with a reconciliation between the King and the Prince of Wales, and with the downfall of Bernstorff, the Duchess of Kendal, whose power and influence were then at their height, was from whatever motive staunch to the English ministers [1].

The name of Bernstorff is by far the most prominent among those of the Hanoverian advisers of George I during his occupancy of the British throne; but perhaps precedence ought to be allowed to Bothmer, who came to England some years before his colleague, and held out there for twelve years after him. Hans Caspar von Bothmer had in the service of George William of Celle, the friend of William III, after acting as envoy at Vienna, been one of the plenipotentiaries at the Congress of Ryswyk. He was subsequently for a time envoy at the Court of Lewis XIV; and after the passing of the Act of Settlement and the advent to the British throne of Queen Anne, who at heart shrank from the prospect of the Hanoverian Succession, was chosen as the principal agent for its accomplishment. In view of the known sentiments of the Queen, it had been thought preferable that he should in the first instance occupy a post of observation at the Hague, whither he proceeded in 1702, and whence he materially contributed to the passing of the Acts of 1706, which placed the position of the House of Hanover on so solid a basis; indeed, it was by means of the Act of Regency, which authorised the heir-presumptive to appoint lords justices for the event of the Queen's demise, that with the aid of Bothmer's presence in England, the new *régime* was afterwards actually established. In 1710 the overthrow of the Whigs and the occupation of their places by a government whose attitude towards the Hanover Succession was at least dubious, made it advisable to settle Bothmer as the Elector's envoy at St. James'; and in this post he laboured unintermittently at the prosecution of his task, till in 1714 he

[1] Lady Cowper's *Diary* (1864), p. 145.

brought it to a successful issue. For his exertions to this end were supplemented, rather than interrupted, by his endeavours as plenipotentiary at Utrecht, which were so far successful that, though the Hanoverian Succession was not recognised in the instrument of peace, a guarantee of it was introduced into one of the Barrier Treaties (the third, of 1715). Placed in a position of exceptional difficulty and delicacy, he was indeed unable to become a *persona grata* either to the Queen or to her ministers ; for a few weeks before her death we find Marshal Schulemburg writing to Leibniz that Bothmer, although a man of merit and probity, and well qualified as a negotiator, was detested by both her and them [1]. But he managed to hold his own, and to avoid such blunders as that of the demand of the Writ into which Schütz allowed himself to be hurried, or what might have proved the still graver step of adopting Marlborough's advice, and anticipating events by landing Dutch and Hanoverian troops. When the crisis came at last, Bothmer played a part of conspicuous importance. On the morning of the day when the Council whose decision settled the situation assembled, a great meeting was held at his house ; when Queen Anne had breathed her last, he actively co-operated in the proclamation of King George I by the lords justices ; and he earned the thanks—or at least he deserved them—of men of all parties by burning the papers left by the Queen in her private cabinet [2]. Bothmer's secretary took to Hanover the news of the accomplished fact ; and on the King's arrival in England, was looked upon as the chief disposer of places. 'The Forreigners,' writes Peter Wentworth, himself both a Whig and an office-seeker, 'tho' they pretend to have nothing to do with the English affairs, yet from the top to the bottom they have a great stroak in recommending Persons that are fit to serve his Majesty; most, nay all the addresses are made to Mons. Bothmar, he having been so long in England, and is supposed to know all the English. There are,' he archly adds,

<hr/>

[1] J. M. Kemble, *State Papers and Correspondence, &c.* (1857), p. 512.

[2] Bodemann, *Ilten*, p. 159, fiom a MS. in the writing of the younger Ilten.

'people wicked enough to suggest that way is made by some to these Persons by money [1].'

Archdeacon Coxe, who it must be allowed is herein quite true to sentiments freely expressed by Sir Robert Walpole himself, has been more or less followed by other English historical writers in lumping 'ministers' with 'mistresses and favourites,' and writing them down as greedy, like the rest of the venal crew, of 'private emoluments' and 'concealed advantages,' since the Act of Settlement had excluded them from British official rank, and had shut the door of the House of Lords in their faces. Yet, unless the fact be thought conclusive that both Bernstorff and Bothmer amassed considerable wealth, the evidence as to the mode in which they acquired it is extremely scanty. As to Bothmer, I perceive no proof that, after the first great rush was over, during which he stood between the King and the office-seekers, he busied himself with the distribution of patronage. Undoubtedly, while the siege lasted, its rigour was excessive, and it is necessary to go through certain portions of the *Robethon Correspondence* in the British Museum in order to form a conception of the extent and variety of the applications made to Bothmer and transmitted by him through Robethon for the royal approval. Some of these refer to the highest offices of State, others to mere Court appointments [2]. Bothmer, who at the time of the accession was nearly a sexagenarian, had virtually reached the climax of his career when the task to which its chief endeavours had been devoted was achieved; and this was acknowledged in 1715 by his being created a Count of the Holy Roman Empire—a significant testimony of Imperial goodwill towards a success so largely due to him. He

---

[1] *The Wentworth Papers*, ed. J. J. Cartwright (1883), p. 427.

[2] Among these, it is pleasant to think, was very probably now or at a later date included the appointment of one of the most charming among the Maids of Honour at the Court of the Princess of Wales—Mary Lepel, afterwards Lady Hervey. She seems to have owed her nomination to the post to the influence of Bothmer, Bernstorff, and the Dowager Duchess of Marlborough; and to have herself sprung from a Mecklenburg, or at all events a Baltic family—not, as Croker thought, from one settled in the Channel Islands. (See *Diary of the First Earl of Bristol*, vol. iv. pp. 287 scqq.).

continued, while holding the mainly ornamental position of Hanoverian envoy in London, together with a non-resident Privy Councillorship, to devote himself closely to foreign affairs. Although they are constantly found acting together, and seem ordinarily to have been guided by the same principles of political conduct, the influence of Bothmer would seem to have waned as that of Bernstorff rose to its height; indeed, in an unsigned letter from Paris in the *Robethon Correspondence* belonging to the year 1718[1] it is roundly asserted that 'Bothmer has but little influence, and it all belongs to M. de Bernstorff.' Yet we know on the authority of a M.S. which in all probability proceeded from Bothmer's own pen, that he took a very direct and noticeable part in the negotiations for the Quadruple Alliance in 1718; and both before and after this date we find him active in the conduct of foreign affairs. In the transactions which ended in August, 1719, with the conclusion of the alliance with Prussia, Bothmer supported the policy of Stanhope against that of Bernstorff, who was bitterly opposed to it. But although he continued down to his death in 1732 to occupy a house in Downing Street (the present official residence of the First Lord of the Treasury[2]), it may be concluded that for some time previous to his death at nearly eighty years of age he must have ceased taking any prominent part in public affairs. He left behind him a very large landed estate in Mecklenburg, together with considerable personal property[3].

In character and disposition Bothmer, whom a contemporary (Ilten) credits with *une humeur douce et bienfaisante*—a description not belied by the letters remaining from his hand—must have been very unlike the foremost of his colleagues, the guiding spirit of the so-called Hanoverian *junta*, the celebrated Baron Andreas Gottlieb von Bernstorff. We need not attach very much importance to the casual utterances of those free-spoken ladies, the favourite niece of the old Electress Sophia and the more discreet but equally quick-witted wife of her grandson. For if the Duchess of Orleans[4] and the Princess of Wales (after-

---

[1] Vol. x. p. 70.   [2] Horace Walpole's *Letters*, vol. i. p. 181 note.

[3] Vehse, *Die Höfe d. Hauses Mecklenburg*, vol. ii. pp. 181–3.

[4] Id., *Die Höfe d. Hauses Braunschweig*, vol. i. p. 221.

wards Queen Caroline[1]) were at one in their vituperation of
Bernstorff, the Princess was also fain to call Bothmer a knave,
and—for that matter—Robethon another[2]. But there are other
indications that he at times gave free expression to the asperity
which was in his nature, and the colleague just cited states it to
have been made an accusation against him that he was *peu
courtisan*. He was certainly well hated in the course of his
career, and numerous aspersions have been cast on him in the
literature of memoirs. But the part played by him in contemporary history was of sufficient importance to warrant the
assertion that he will not be finally judged by the inconsiderate-
ness which was at times resented in his manners, nor even by
the admixture of personal motives which was at times thought
discernible in his political action.

The autobiography of Bernstorff printed by Dr. Köcher from
the MS. in the Hanover archives[3], and reaching up to the year
1716, covers less than a dozen pages, and is couched in a laconic
style of ultra-official dryness. But his life had contained at least
one passionate passage in his youth, and in his later days he
was certainly not in the habit of toning down the strength of his
opinions as to men and things. Bernstorff, as we shall have to
remember when adverting in our next lecture to the intervention
of the Czar in the Mecklenburg question, was a landed noble in
Mecklenburg-Schwerin, and took a leading part in the early
stages of the quarrel between his Order and their territorial
prince, Duke Charles Lewis, which was carried on for a period
of something more than half a century; but he had quitted the
Ducal Court many years before, having fallen in love with the
Duke's first consort, a lady of the French house of Montmorency.
At Celle, where he took service under Duke George William,
he however married the daughter of Chancellor Schütz, described
in his son-in-law's *Autobiography* as 'one of the greatest and
most capable ministers that he had ever known.' He took part
in the campaigns of the Brunswick-Lüneburg troops against

[1] Lady Cowper's *Diary*, p. 79.
[2] *Ib.*, p. 87.
[3] *Die Selbstbiographie des Ministers A. G. von Bernstorff.* (*Pro-
gramm des Kaiser Wilhelm's Gymnasiums in Hanover*, 1877.)

France in 1674 and 1675 ; and having soon afterwards, on the death of his father-in-law, assumed the direction of affairs at Celle, passed thence in 1705 into the service of the Elector George Lewis at Hanover. In 1709, on the death of Count Platen, the husband of the notorious Countess Platen, Bernstorff became chief minister. He had taken a leading part in the negotiations with Portland which secured to William of Orange the armed support of the Brunswick-Lüneburg dukes on the occasion of his expedition to England in 1688. But perhaps the note-worthiest feature in his political activity during the period preceding the accession of the House of Hanover to the British throne was the suspicious vigilance with which he strove to guard against the ambition of his master's two most important neighbours, the King of Denmark and the Elector of Branden-burg. Against Brandenburg he cherished an unextinguishable aversion; and while jealousy of Prussia was one of the most potent, as it was one of the most enduring factors in the dynastic policy of the House of Hanover through a great part of the earlier half of the eighteenth century, that jealousy was incarnate in Bernstorff.

In 1714 he had accompanied George I to England as the recognised chief of his German councillors, and this position he maintained till the time of his political overthrow. There can be no mistake as to the contemptuous dislike with which he regarded the conditions of political life that he found existing in his master's new kingdom, nor as to his belief that it behoved him to set them right, so far as in him lay, by a continuous exertion of his own personal influence over the King. In one of the few passages in his *Autobiography* where he gives the rein to his private feelings, he recalls the infinite importu-nities and vexations which had to be borne during the process of forming a Court and a government at the time of the King's accession, and refers to the incredible multitude of applicants who imagined themselves 'fit for anything and everything.' Of his varied and indefatigable activity during the first five or six years of the reign no more convincing evidence can be required than is furnished in the *Diary* of Lady Cowper, who, like her husband, was on very friendly terms with

Bernstorff; indeed, the appointment of Whigs to all the higher
offices of State was largely due to the historical narrative drawn
up by Lord Cowper when a lord justice, and laid before the
King by Bernstorff. In the *Diary* we find the latter not only
busying himself concerning all sorts of appointments in and about
the Court, but also interfering as to nominations on the Bench
of Judges, and freely giving his opinion on matters whether of
administration or of legislation. He was a consistent upholder
of the Whigs, notwithstanding the distrust of their party fostered
in the Prince and Princess of Wales; but his long-sustained
endeavour to remain the recognised agent of the royal will and
exponent of its ultimate decisions split on the rock of Townshend
and Walpole's determination to maintain the responsibility of
the King's ministers. There can be little doubt as to the
unscrupulousness of the procedure adopted by Walpole in order
to break Bernstorff's influence in 1720; and whether or not
Lord Cowper and Lady Mary Wortley Montagu were justified
in asserting that his wholesale charges of corruption against the
Hanoverian minister might have been made to recoil on his
own head [1], I am disposed to conclude that much of the popular
prejudice excited against Bernstorff was the result of exaggera-
tion, if not of invention. His influence at Court was necessarily
limited, and already in 1716 he experienced a rebuff on
attempting to carry through the King's wishes as to restricting
the powers of the Prince of Wales and joining others with him
in the Commission of Regency during the King's absence from
England. But his ascendancy was most marked and enduring
in the sphere of foreign affairs, as is shown by the great
deference paid to him and to his influence upon the progress of
European politics by many of Robethon's correspondents, both
English and foreign. That in 1715-6 we should find the
Imperial Resident stating foreign business to be in the hands of
the Hanoverian ministers is of course by no means surprising,
for serious home troubles were then absorbing much of the
attention of the cabinet. In December, 1716, Bothmer, writing

[1] See Lady Cowper, p. 134; and cf. Lady Mary Wortley Montagu's
State of Affairs, &c., in *Works*, ed. Lord Wharncliffe (3rd ed.), vol. i.
p. 139.

from London, expresses a strong wish for Bernstorff's return with the King; and in the following month Cadogan at the Hague represents the Grand Pensionary as most anxious for an interview with him at Amsterdam on his way, to discuss the affairs of the North[1]. In the period of the Triple and Quadruple Alliance, when English diplomacy was most active and energetic, Bernstorff's influence upon our foreign business is (so far as I can judge) even more noticeable than before, and it rises to its height during the earlier, at least, of the years (1717–20) of Stanhope's 'German ministry.' Yet this influence was by no means always palatable to Stanhope, any more than it had been to his predecessor; and in one important respect he resisted it successfully. It may very well be that the mortification inflicted on Bernstorff in 1720, by the achievement without his knowledge of a reconciliation between the King and the Prince of Wales, was partly due to a desire for revenge on the part of Stanhope, whose foreign policy had been seriously hampered, without being effectually thwarted, by Bernstorff's irrepressible hatred of Prussia[2], and that this revenge was wreaked by him with the aid of the Duchess of Kendal. In the summer of 1720 Bernstorff once more accompanied George I to Hanover, but when in November the South Sea catastrophe obliged the King to return to England, the old minister (he was now in his seventy-second year) thought it more prudent to

[1] *Robethon Papers,* vol. viii. pp. 360 and 370.

[2] 'I conjure M. de Bernstorff,' the Abbé Dubois writes to Robethon in 1718, 'to sacrifice or dissimulate whatever dislike (*éloignement*) he may have for the House of Prussia,' and to consent to an alliance with her which would frustrate the Swedish hopes of a Northern League. Bernstorff had kept Prussia out of the Triple Alliance, but failed in his opposition to the treaty, actually concluded in August, 1719, between Great Britain and Prussia, with the object of bringing about a satisfactory peace between each of these powers and Sweden. (Cf. *Lecture III.*) His conduct in this matter was the more open to unfavourable comment, since it was supposed to be swayed by personal interest, in reference to certain villages owned by his family that were in the treaty ceded by Prussia to Hanover. (Cf. Droysen, *Geschichte der preussischen Politik,* vol. ii. part 2, pp. 260 seqq.; and Stanhope, *u. s.,* vol. ii. Appendix, p. lxxx.)

remain behind. The last words of his autobiography stand on record as a jotting which he never elaborated : ' Why in the year 1720 I did not go to England.' A new period in the history of the reign now commenced with the readmission into the government of Walpole and Townshend. Between 1720 and 1723, when he actually quitted, or was dismissed from office, Bernstorff appears to have played no prominent part either in foreign or other public affairs. He was probably for the greater part of this period resident in Hanover ; for it was here that about 1722 he tried one more fall with the leading English ministers, in opposition to whom he supported Carteret and the supple minister-resident, Sir Luke Schaub, whom Carteret had placed at Paris, in their attempt to push the intrigue of the La Vrillière dukedom. The scheme practically fell through, and, even before Carteret's control of foreign affairs, Bernstorff's public life came to an end. He died in London in 1726, a year before his master. Like Bothmer, he left his wealth to an only daughter, from whom the eminent Danish statesmen bearing his name were directly descended.

None of the other Hanoverians who accompanied King George I to England exercised a personal influence upon the administration or policy of the kingdom of which any traces remain. Baron (afterwards Count) von Schlitz-Görz very soon returned to Hanover, where he remained a member of the ministry, and held the Presidency of the Exchequer Chamber till his death in 1728. Lady Mary Wortley Montagu describes him as a ' plain, sincere and unambitious man [1]' ; but he seems, possibly with an eye to the inclinations of the Prince of Wales, to have entered into relations with some of the Tory leaders. His withdrawal from London is significant of the ascendancy of Bernstorff, to whom he had opposed himself already in earlier days, when his rival had taken so active a part in promoting the English Succession. Probably he was not far from the truth in excusing himself to the enterprising John Ker of Kersland, as unable to do anything for him, when that worthy came over from Hanover with an admirable letter from Leibniz, protesting against its being thought possible that German ministers should

[1] *Account of the Court of George I*, in *Works*, i. 125.

meddle in English affairs. Bernstorff and Bothmer, he said, were the only foreigners who ignored the precept—or, as he might have put the point, who ignored it with effect[1].

The younger Hattorf (Philip), when he went over in lieu of his father with the King in 1714, exercised secretarial rather than ministerial functions, and only later became the regular minister in attendance. His ultimate appointment is noteworthy as the solitary instance during the period of the Personal Union of a leading position in the Hanoverian government being held by an official not born a member of the ancient nobility; but Hattorf, as we shall see when speaking of the reign of George II, was a man of exceptional ability and tact.

I should mention no other name in the present connexion, since it is beyond my purpose to speak either of the ministers of George I at home in Hanover, or of the officials around the King-Elector's person, among whom certain conspicuous connexions were as a matter of course amply represented. But it might seem strange to pass by one indefatigable agent, whose influence upon the progress of the affairs of George I continued for several years after he had become King of Great Britain. Strictly speaking, of course, Jean de Robethon ought not to be mentioned side by side with the Hanoverian ministers and employees; but he came to England as an old official of the new Sovereign; nor was he, so far as I know, ever admitted into the British public service. He is variously addressed as 'Domestic Secretary and Privy Councillor,' 'Privy Councillor of Ambassage,' and 'Aulic Councillor'; and I have not come across his name as recipient of a British official salary. He had no connexion whatever with the Hanoverian Privy Council, or even with the London office. Yet he has been justly described[2] as the very soul of George I's diplomatic chancery, and among all the politicians of the day he was beyond all doubt the most closely trusted by both Hanoverian statesmen and English and foreign diplomatists.

Like Bernstorff himself, and like Fabrice, the father of two valued official servants of George I, Robethon had passed into

---

[1] See *Memoirs of John Ker of Kersland* (3rd ed., 1727), vol. i. pp. 100 seqq. [2] By Pauli.

the electoral service out of that of George William of Celle. But, unlike them, he had previously been in the service of William III, having entered it, perhaps on being driven into exile by the Revocation of the Edict of Nantes, perhaps at a rather later date, since he is known to have been naturalised in England in 1693. He accompanied Portland as secretary to Paris on his celebrated embassy after the Peace of Ryswyk, and in 1698 was established as private secretary to the King himself. During Queen Anne's reign he was actively engaged in the long diplomatic campaign for carrying through the Succession of the House of Brunswick, and when Bothmer was sent to England, for a time took his place as electoral envoy at the Hague. He then returned to Hanover, the notion of sending him to London having been abandoned—probably quite as much because of his want of birth and breeding, as because of his being certain to be unacceptable to the Tories in power. From the accession of King George onwards, Robethon became at London what he had been at Hanover—the chief confidential agent of the policy guided by Bernstorff and Bothmer. He was also employed to translate, and probably on occasion to draft, royal proclamations, speeches to Parliament, and the like. But just as he had been much more than the mere draughtsman of the ideas and projects of others in the Succession correspondence, a larger proportion of which had beyond a doubt fallen to his share than to that of any other political agent, so the ministers of the new *régime*, diplomatists like Stair, and leading foreign statesmen such as Dubois, concurred in treating him as a personality to be reckoned with. His supreme claim to importance lay in his being known to possess the complete confidence of Bernstorff[1].

---

[1] The statement of John Ker of Kersland (*Memoirs, u. s.*), that he had been advised of five hundred guineas to Robethon being the only way of securing Bernstorff's good word, need (like other statements from the same source) not be taken *au pied de la lettre*. More to the point perhaps is Lord Strafford's request to Robethon to correct a report unfavourable to the Ambassador's reputation for discretion, and supplicating him to bring this disclaimer to the notice of Bernstorff and 'your other ministers' (*Robethon Correspondence*, vol. vi. p. 378).

The British ministers unmistakeably regarded his activity with the reverse of goodwill ; but the contemptuous abuse that flowed so easily from the lips of prejudiced contemporaries need not have been accepted as decisive by sober modern historians. The *Robethon Correspondence* in the British Museum furnishes abundant evidence of his political knowledge and insight, and of the important share belonging to him in many of the chief political transactions of the first six years, or thereabouts, of the reign of George I. A perusal of many of these papers has convinced me of the justice of the estimate of Robethon's powers and services given by Mr. J. F. Chance in an admirable recent contribution to the *English Historical Review* [1].

---

[1] Vol. xiii. No. 49, for January, 1898. Robethon seems to have been excluded from any share in public affairs from about 1720, having supported Bernstorff against Stanhope in the attempt to prevent the treaty with Prussia. He died April 17, 1722.

LECTURE III

THE FOREIGN POLICY OF GEORGE I (1714–21)

IN briefly commenting on some of the transactions of our
foreign policy in the reign of George I, into which his
interests or sympathies as Elector of Hanover more or less
distinctly entered, I shall perforce have to treat the spheres of
that policy to some extent apart from one another. Yet,
of course, even a far less intelligent conduct of foreign
affairs than that which makes this reign so noticeable an
epoch of our diplomatic history could not, while acting in
one sphere, have ignored the rest. Within the European
range of relations to which the attention of our statesmen
was still as a rule restricted, they were constantly reminded
of the mutual influence of political movements far distant
from one another in origin; one of the chief disturbing
forces of the period, the ambition of Spain guided by Alberoni, sought to accomplish its end by utilising the wrath
of the Swedish King, and we find George I promising the
Emperor to let the British fleet winter in the Mediterranean, although it would be of the last importance to him
to send part of it into the Baltic[1]. It would be interesting
to know to what extent the combination of questions
and issues *primâ facie* remote from one another was
impeded by the distribution, habitual at this time, of the
management of business between two Secretaries of State,
so that for instance the Secretary for the Southern Depart-

[1] *Record Office, Regencies*, vol. xii (August 14, 1719).

ment attended to the affairs of France and Spain, and the Secretary of the Northern to those of the Empire and the Scandinavian North. But no arrangement could have been better calculated to produce misunderstandings between the two Secretaries themselves, more especially when the Crown was swayed by counsels more favourable to the policy and conduct of one of the pair than to those of his colleague.

In the case of Townshend and Stanhope we know that such a misunderstanding actually arose, and ended in open rupture. Yet the choice of each of these statesmen as Secretary had approved itself to the King's Hanoverian advisers. Townshend indeed, the Northern Secretary, owed his appointment, if Lady Mary Wortley Montagu is to be trusted, to Robethon's remembrance of courtesies received from him when Ambassador at the Hague in Queen Anne's time; this was a passport to Bernstorff's goodwill; and Bothmer had likewise interested himself in Townshend's behalf[1]. Lady Mary, in her cynical way, implies that it was Townshend's docility which carried him successfully through the first part of his public career; but, as not unfrequently happens with its lively authoress, the suggestion conveyed is unjustly contemptuous, for nothing distinguished this statesman so much as his high and unyielding sense of honour. Neither, however, in the measure of his powers nor in the lustre of his public services, can he be said to have equalled his fellow-Secretary Stanhope, whose appointment was more than justified by conspicuous services to the State, and above all to the alliance with the House of Austria, so that he could

---

[1] *Robethon Correspondence*, vol. vi. p. 405 (September 11, 1714). Bothmer was troubled to find Sunderland after all desirous of the office. He was actually appointed to it in April, 1717, after Townshend's resignation.—Coxe (*Life of Sir Robert Walpole*, ed. 18, vol. i. p. 113) says that Townshend had ' secured and governed Bothmer before the King's arrival '; but this may possibly not be altogether the right way of putting it.

hardly fail sooner or later to establish his ascendancy in the conduct of British foreign policy under the House of Hanover.

At the commencement of the new reign, general attention was still fixed upon the settlement of our relations with the Power against which we had waged the long war that had but recently been brought to a close. The Peace had been vehemently condemned by the party which had now recovered the control of the administration, nor had its conditions been satisfactorily carried out by France. Following traditions that seemed unlikely to be buried so long as the old King survived, her attitude remained steadily provocative; nothing seemed capable of altering it but another war ; and towards such a war the new British Government could not, without apprehension, feel itself drifting[1]. For the Grand Alliance was a thing of the past ; and if Great Britain was to enter into a new conflict, she ought at least to be sure of the support of her old allies the United Provinces and the Emperor. But while the latter had been alienated from Great Britain by the Peace of Utrecht, he was at issue with the Dutch about their so-called barrier of fortresses in the Austrian Netherlands, which was as irksome to Charles VI in the second decade of the century as it was to Joseph II in the ninth. However, an end was put to the prospect of a renewal of hostilities with France by the death of Louis XIV (September 1, 1715), and the establishment in the sole Regency of the Duke of Orleans, the maternal kinsman of George I. The King's own throne was speedily strengthened by the overthrow of the Rebellion of the '15, to effect which Lord Stair had suggested the shipping of seven or eight battalions of Hanoverian troops

---

[1] A few weeks before the death of Louis XIV Robethon was informed from Paris that England was then generally believed to be on the point of recommencing war against France. (*Robethon Correspondence*, vol. vii. p. 79.)

from Bremen, Hamburg, and Stade[1]: but we had no treaty
with the Electorate analogous to that with the Dutch, and the
conclusion of a subsidy-treaty *ad hoc* was probably thought
inexpedient under the circumstances. The improved position
of the new *régime* in Great Britain showed itself in the friend-
liness displayed towards it by the Emperor. Not only was
his assent given to a new Barrier Treaty, more favourable to
the Dutch than its predecessor, mediated by the British
Government; but he was in 1716 prevailed upon to conclude a treaty with Great Britain herself, in which each
Power guaranteed the possessions of the other. This treaty
having been concluded by George I as King of Great
Britain only, and not as Elector of Hanover also, it followed
that, notwithstanding certain apprehensions on the Austrian
side, no guarantee of Hanoverian possessions could be involved in it. None of the Hanoverian ministers therefore
appended his signature to the instrument[2], whatever part they
may have taken in the preceding negotiations; and thus no
complication was introduced into an arrangement which
materially strengthened the European influence of Great
Britain. It was at this very season—the summer of 1716—
that King George I, for the first time since his accession to
the British throne, visited his Electorate, and that Stanhope,
who accompanied him as Secretary of State, contrived *en
route* to prepare, by the earliest of his 'unbuttoned' conver-
sations with the Abbé Dubois, that further developement of
our foreign policy of which friendship with France and a
thorough understanding with the Emperor constituted the
joint conditions.

To this we may return a little later. While at the beginning of the reign, for the Powers that had taken part in the

[1] *Robethon Correspondence*, vol. iii. p. 320.
[2] Michael, *Englische Geschichte im* 18. *Jahrhundert*, vol. i. (1896),
p. 675.

war of the Spanish Succession, no problem of European politics could vie in importance with that of the relations between the chief of those Powers themselves, another war was still in progress in which hitherto none of them had become involved. The so-called Northern War had been to all intents and purposes localised; but would such a restriction of the conflict continue possible, after the House of Hanover, which had recently so to speak acquired a direct interest in its progress, had succeeded to the British throne? Together with Stanhope, Bernstorff, with Robethon by his side, accompanied King George on the journey to Hanover which in spite of so many and serious obstacles he had persisted in undertaking. Bothmer remained behind in London, in constant communication, as the Robethon Correspondence shows, with his colleagues at Hanover; nor can there have been any time in his reign when a greater number of influences combined to urge upon George I the prosecution of interests which he made no secret of having particularly at heart.

The day of Pultawa, while checking the victorious career of Charles XII of Sweden, had neither overthrown his power nor broken his spirit. But his long delay in the dominions of the Sultan, who was in the end altogether to disappoint his hopes, had enabled the adversaries against whom he had so successfully contended in the first nine years of the war, to partition among them the outer circle of his dominions. The Nemesis of an aggrandisement for which he was not responsible, after being by his genius for a time averted from his kingdom, had at last descended upon it, and the conquests which, from the Peace of Westphalia to that of Roeskilde, had swelled the territories of the great northern Power were torn from her one by one.

Among these were what are commonly called the Duchies of Bremen and Verden, or, more accurately, the Duchy of Bremen and the Principality of Verden. The Duchy of

Bremen consisted of the former dominions of the Archbishop of Bremen, which after the Reformation had been held, together with the See, by princes of the neighbouring houses, including that of Brunswick-Lüneburg, but which in the Peace of Westphalia had passed as a secular duchy into the possession of the Swedish Crown. (The city of Bremen maintained its immediacy to the Empire, but this was disputed by Sweden and afterwards by Hanover, who however recognised it in 1731.) The bishopric of Verden had actually formed part of the dominions of Henry the Lion; it had then become immediate, and in the Peace of Westphalia had been made over to Sweden as a secular principality. It results that the House of Hanover could pretend to no claim to these territories (which by the way included the two cathedral churches in the free cities of Bremen and Hamburg), but that it had a historical connexion or association with them. A glance at the map will show that together they command the course of the Weser from something like twenty miles above Bremen to its mouth, and that of the Elbe to its mouth from the near neighbourhood of Hamburg; on the further side of the river lies Holstein. Above Hamburg the Elbe formed the northern boundary of the Brunswick-Lüneburg dominions.

The proprietorship of the Bremen-Verden lands was therefore a matter of consequence to the Elector of Hanover. The princes of the House to which he belonged had felt deeply aggrieved by the settlement made in the matter by the Peace of Westphalia; and both before and after that treaty they had jealously watched the aggressive policy of Sweden. But of late their vigilance had been directed less against Sweden than against her inveterate enemy Denmark, whose appetite for territory they had more reason for fearing. When therefore, in 1712, the Danish King Frederick IV sought to avenge the humiliations of Travendahl by occupying Bremen and

Verden, and in 1713 with Saxon aid partially carried out his purpose, the situation became one in which it must be allowed that some sort of intervention on the part of Hanover hardly remained avoidable. Moreover, her mediation had been invoked by her near neighbour, the Duke of Holstein-Gottorp (the nephew of Charles XII), whose territories the Danes were likewise overrunning. They were indeed defeated by a Swedish force; but after this had been obliged to surrender to a combined army of the Powers in alliance against Sweden, they once more established themselves in the Bremen territory. In order, therefore, to hold some sort of security against a complete Danish occupation in the first instance, as well as to guard his own future interests, the Elector George Lewis hereupon occupied Verden and Ottenburg (just across the Bremen boundary). Then, while opening negotiations with Denmark as to the settlement of their respective claims, he ranged himself definitively on the side of the enemies of Sweden by sending a Hanoverian contingent to their army, now in Pomerania. These steps had been taken shortly before the accession of the Elector of Hanover to the British throne; and there could be no question but that they must lead to consequences of serious moment for Great Britain, so soon as the Personal Union should have been accomplished.

Up to this time, whatever friction might have arisen from the state of shipping and trade in the Baltic, Great Britain had held aloof from any intervention in the Northern complication, and taken no part in the proceedings of the adversaries of Charles XII, either before or after Pultawa. When, late in November, 1714, the Swedish King reached Stralsund, after his wonderful ride across Europe, very pleasant compliments were interchanged between him and the British Minister accredited to him (Jefferyes), whom he requested to transmit his congratulations on King George's accession through Bernstorff—though the diplomatist thought it more proper to forward them through Townshend[1]. But soon Charles was better informed. Almost at the very time of his arrival at Stralsund, a treaty of mutual guarantee had been arranged at Berlin by the Hanoverian Privy Councillor Eltz, one of the most devoted servants of his master (indeed he is called the King's *âme damnée* by Ilten), between Great Britain and Prussia, the Power most vitally interested in the extrusion of Sweden from the Empire[2]. Next, it was determined to take quick advantage of the apprehensions excited in the Danish Court by the news of Charles' imminent return[3], and of the uneasy feeling there that he might contrive to detach George I from the Anti-Swedish league, by voluntarily ceding Bremen and Verden to him[4]. In truth, this would have been a sagacious move, although not one after the manner of Charles XII. The negotiations which ensued between Hanover and Denmark ended in a formal alliance between them in May, 1715, for the expulsion of the Swedes from the Empire, and in the cession in June by Denmark to Hanover of Bremen and Verden, whose Estates in the October following did homage to the Elector at Stade. Five years later, Sweden, no longer a great Power, formally ceded these territories to their Hanoverian occupant, receiving in return a compensation of 1,185,000 dollars.

[1] *Robethon Papers*, vol. vi. pp. 538-9. It is curious to find Bothmer, as late as August, writing to Robethon in a sympathetic tone as to the difficulties in the way of Charles XII's return.

[2] Droysen, *u. s.*, vol. iv. Part ii. pp. 201-2.

[3] In October, 1714, Fabrice reported the King of Denmark to be more tractable. (*Robethon Correspondence*, vol. vi. pp. 478-9.)

[4] The fears of Frederick IV on this score are mentioned by his biographer Hoyer. (Herrmann, *Geschichte Russlands*, vol. iii. p. 491.) Similar information had reached Jefferyes from the Swedish legation at Vienna. (*Robethon Correspondence*, *u. s.*, p. 540.) But if Charles entertained any such intention, he must have very speedily abandoned it.

This is the Hanoverian aspect of the matter. A considerable province, speaking relatively, was added to the Electorate, in extent falling not very far short of its previous dominions, and rounding them off appropriately on the North towards Holstein, as it was intended East Frisia should at some future date round them off towards the Netherlands [1]. An ancestral sentiment had been gratified by the incorporation of lands formerly connected with the House of Brunswick; some share in the commercial prosperity of Hamburg and Bremen might be expected to accrue to the inhabitants of the marsh-lands between the estuaries of the two great North Sea rivers; and a ray or two of the faint glow of patriotism evoked by the displacement of the Scandinavian intruder would fall upon the princely house to whose action it was due.

But during the six years which were required for carrying this design to a successful conclusion, much had happened showing it to be fraught with less acceptable results for the Great Power with which the Hanoverian Electorate was now associated in a Personal Union. Inasmuch as the correspondence in the Record Office bearing on some of these transactions is supplemented by the very voluminous collection of Carteret's Letters and Despatches in the British Museum, there is at least evidence enough to throw light upon what may be called the British side of the question.

Before the proceedings of George I with regard to Bremen and Verden could have entered as a factor into the relations between Great Britain and Sweden, the danger of an outbreak of hostilities had already been near at hand. This seems to be placed beyond all doubt by a statement transmitted by the Lord Justices to the King on August 7, previously to his arrival. From this document it appears

---

[1] The hereditary compact (*Erbverbrüderung*) between Ernest Augustus and Christian Eberhard of East Frisia had been concluded in 1691.

that four men-of-war had been sent into the Baltic to provide for the safety of our merchantmen there; and that our resident at Stockholm (Jackson) having expressed his opinion that if a chance were given to the Swedish squadron it would attack the British, the officer in command (Captain Hamilton) had been furnished with instructions to return to the Thames if danger were to be apprehended[1]. As a matter of fact, during the course of the Northern War Swedish privateers had captured a large number of British merchantmen, on the plea that they were carrying contraband of war into the Russian ports, over which Sweden had established a blockade. though doubtless to a large extent on paper only. The damages suffered by English trade were estimated at nearly £70,000[2]; and it may safely be concluded that the great body of these losses had been inflicted before the occupation of Verden, and that no thought of this proceeding entered into the naval votes passed by Parliament in the earlier part of the year 1715. In the month of June of this year a British fleet under Sir John Norris anchored in the Sound, where it found a Dutch squadron already in waiting; and by the close of the month the two fleets safely convoyed a large number of English and Dutch merchant vessels to their respective ports. So far it cannot be said that these proceedings, whatever gloss might be put upon them by interested parties, had been carried beyond the necessary requirements of the case.

The liberality of the naval votes which had preceded the despatch of the fleet shows it to have been approved by

[1] *Record Office, Regencies*, vol. xi (1713-4): Secretary Bromley 'to the King,' from Whitehall, August 7, 1714. He is instructed to say that the Swedes, whose men-of-war and privateers daily seized British ships or effects, gave out that these practices were intended to suppress the supply of their enemies with necessaries of war through British ships, in contravention of existing treaties.

[2] Campbell's *Naval History of Great Britain* (1813), vol. iv. p. 130.

Parliamentary and public opinion ; nor is any trace discoverable of a belief or suspicion in England that the fleet was intended to bring hostile pressure to bear upon Sweden in connivance with the Powers allied against her. Only a few months before the accession of King George I the British Government had actively exerted itself on behalf of Sweden, and Norris' instructions for the expedition of 1715 appear to have borne entirely upon reprisals for the Swedish excesses against British trade, committed more especially by the privateers licensed by royal edict. But in the course of the summer the intention of utilising the fleet for the furtherance of the understanding between Hanover and Denmark, or in other words for the purposes of league of aggression against Sweden, becomes more and more transparent. In August Norris' squadron sails from Copenhagen as the vanguard of a united armada of British, Russian, and Danish men-of-war, and the Hanoverian agents busy themselves in pledging their master as to its employment. In London Bernstorff assures the Prussian Resident Bonet that the British movements in the Baltic are in point of fact directed to a twofold end. At Berlin the Hanoverian minister Heusch requests King Frederick William I to content himself with a verbal undertaking that Norris' fleet shall be used to support the combination against Sweden, since a written engagement would have to go through the hands of the British ministers [1]. As for Norris, he had at first hoped to induce the Dutch admiral to join him in offensive action against the Swedes [2]; and though when met by a refusal he exhibited an access of caution, he kept the Swedish fleet shut up in Carlscrona by the movements of his fleet during the latter part of his stay

[1] Michael, vol. i. pp. 717–8.
[2] See the despatches of Sir John Norris calendared in the Eleventh Report of the *Historical MSS. Commission, Appendix,* Part IV (1887). pp. 89 seqq.

in the Baltic, and more especially by leaving eight ships
behind him there in September to co-operate with the Danes.
Thus, the immediate object of the allies, the capture of
Stralsund and Rügen from the Swedes, was in 1715 successfully accomplished; and Hanoverian troops formed part of
the besieging forces to which, in the month of April of the
following year, Wismar was surrendered by the Swedes
as the last place still in their occupation on German
soil[1].

Still, however, Great Britain had not positively engaged in
the struggle. In the spring of 1716 Norris was once more
in the Baltic, with instructions resembling those of the preceding year, but enlarged by suitable general phraseology.
He was also commissioned—nor unfitly, since, though laconic
in his style, he holds a distinguished place among British
diplomatist-admirals—to address a letter to King Charles XII
urging him to make peace with his adversaries, and offering
the mediation of Great Britain for the purpose. But on
receiving this letter Charles returned it unopened, prohibiting
his Senate at the same time from replying to a parallel
memorandum addressed to it by the British resident.
Charles XII had in fact soon after his arrival at Stralsund
fallen under the influence of Görtz, and if he had ever thought
of a transaction with George I concerning Bremen and Verden,
had now completely abandoned any notion of the kind.
Justly resenting the conduct of the Hanoverian Government,
he had, even before the year 1715 was out, allowed communications to be set on foot with the heads of the Jacobite
insurrection in Scotland. It would be futile to seek for
the origin of Charles XII's wrath in the Baltic trade difficulties, and the self-aggrandising action of the Hanoverian
Government must be held responsible for the introduction
of a new and unwelcome complication into the foreign

[1] Havemann, *u. s.*, vol. iii. p. 497.

relations of Great Britain at a time when they were already full of difficulties. And the menace might have grown to something worse, had not the Swedish invasion of Norway led to the planning of a counter-invasion of Scania, which in its turn obliged Charles to defer any Scottish enterprise. But although the Jacobite broke down hopelessly, unaided by the formidable sword of the Swedish king, his indignation against George I and his government was unmistakeably one of the chief motives determining him to embrace the schemes of Görtz.

Of these schemes the British Government became aware as early as October, 1716, and by the following December, as appears from the Robethon Correspondence, they caused the liveliest apprehensions to our ministers and their friends at the Hague. The starting-point of Görtz's vast design was a reconciliation between Charles XII and the Czar Peter; and this new line of policy opened vistas where figured the versatile and aspiring minister at the head of Spanish affairs, together with Fortune's mendicant, the Pretender, whom the enemies of England had always with them. The discovery of these plans blunted their point for the nonce; but the incidents by which it was accompanied, and especially the arrest of the Swedish Ambassador Count Gyllenborg in London, and that of the British resident (Jackson) at Stockholm by way of reprisal, caused the tension between Sweden and Great Britain to become unbearable. Already in October, 1716, as Bothmer writes to Robethon[1], Swedish privateers in quest of English vessels were sighted close to our coasts; and had it not been for the schism among the Whig leaders which nearly put the Government in a minority on a vote of supply for Baltic requirements, war must have been declared against Sweden at the very time when Charles XII was contemplating a reconciliation with his Russian adversary.

[1] *Robethon Correspondence*, vol. viii. p. 149.

But more than this.   Just when our quarrels with Sweden, embittered by Hanoverian action, seemed on the point of ending in open war, and when the Swedish King was lending his ear to the suggestion that he should throw himself into the arms of Russia, the Hanoverian Government had become involved in a dispute with that Power as well as with Sweden. The Mecklenburg difficulty might be left aside as a typical German quarrel in the circumstances of its origin as well as in those of its endurance; for the echoes of this dispute long outlasted the term of King George I's natural life, and indeed still resounded in the ears of Frederick II of Prussia, when, in 1746, he composed in its original form his *History of his own Times*.   This once famous contention interests us on the present occasion, neither as illustrating the relations of the territorial to the Imperial authority in the period of its decay, nor as exhibiting the relative pertinacity of an unintelligent despotism and of estates inflated with an undue sense of their own consequence.   In itself it was a controversy by which the interests of Great Britain were not in the remotest way affected, and it therefore stands on a quite different footing even from the annexation to Hanover of Bremen and Verden. Yet it exposed Great Britain to the imminent risk of a collision with Russia, who at this moment was seeking either by war or by management to make herself mistress of the Baltic, and turning her face westward to become a member of the European family of nations; and though this collision was actually averted, it helped to determine our attitude towards Russia in the whole question of the settlement of the North, which, after many demonstrations of force and fire, ended in a signal failure of British statesmanship.

Charles Leopold, Duke of Mecklenburg-Schwerin, who is historically not less grotesque a figure than he may be supposed to have been in person, certainly did his utmost to set by the ears the world at large, as well as his own particular dominions. He had inherited a standing quarrel with the knightage or nobility of his duchy—a body which within living memory maintained its reputation for extreme self-consciousness—while he had precipitated another dispute with his capital, Rostock. When, in 1713, he succeeded to his dukedom, the Northern War was still in progress, and Charles Leopold, like many another petty potentate of his day, kept up a standing army, which he gradually raised to 14,000 men, and for which he accordingly needed an increase of contributions. Twelve years previously to his accession the Mecklenburg-Schwerin nobility had resisted the compact (*Schweriner Vergleich*) by which the amount of military contributions had been regulated under his predecessor; and in this protest, to which the extraordinary length of the subsequent dispute gave celebrity, the name at the head of the list was that of the minister of the Elector of Hanover, Andreas Gottlieb von Bernstorff, whose connexion with Mecklenburg has already been noted. Bernstorff's name was, together with those of other protesting landed noblemen, removed from the roll of the Diet; and the suggestion has been repeated with unusual pertinacity that a personal motive influenced the counsels offered by Bernstorff to his Hanoverian master in the ensuing complications. In 1714, the nobility, in reply to the exactions of the Duke, went a step further, and obtained an Imperial rescript intended to protect them against a renewal of such proceedings; but the Duke, after attempting to retort upon his nobles by abolishing the institution of serfdom which was profitable to them as landowners, resorted to a more direct method of coercion. In 1716 he had connected himself with the Muscovite dynasty by marrying a daughter of Ivan, the elder brother of the Czar Peter, and immediately afterwards he induced the Czar to quarter in the recalcitrant duchy the large army with which, in the interests of the alliance against

Sweden, he had undertaken to operate upon the coast of Scania. But this, as was seen just now, was the time of the daring intrigues of Görtz, primarily directed towards bringing about an amicable understanding between Sweden and Russia; and it is not wonderful that suspicion and disunion should have come to prevail among the members of the Anti-Swedish league of which these intrigues stultified the purpose. Denmark was afraid of Russia; Hanover, under the name and style of Great Britain, was seeking to impose her mediation upon the other combatants; and the expedition to Scania was necessarily postponed, after Denmark had refused winter-quarters to the Russian forces, and King George I had with difficulty been prevented from ordering Sir John Norris to give effect to the royal sentiments by means of a *coup de main* against the person of the Czar.

Now undoubtedly the ' Czarish ' occupation of Mecklenburg constituted both an insult to the integrity of the Empire and a danger to the safety of the Hanoverian dominions. If the Imperial authority was thus to be set at defiance, because a hot-brained prince had married into the Muscovite autocrat's family, there was no reason why his soldiery should not flood the territories of his neighbour, with whom he was notoriously on terms the reverse of friendly. But though King George's aversion to the Czar was now intensified into violent hatred, he can scarcely have expected the British ministers to accede to his proposal of dealing with his brother-potentate after a fashion for which it would not have been easy to find recent Western precedents[1]; nor could the violation of the territories of the Empire furnish a sufficient reason for the intervention of a British fleet. Even when, instead of withdrawing his troops from Mecklenburg, the

---

[1] Cellamare's plot for carrying off the Regent of France belongs to the end of 1718.

Czar quartered between 30,000 and 40,000 of them upon his nephew's unlucky subjects, and when the Hanoverian minis- ters were stirring up an anti-Russian agitation throughout the Empire—Bernstorff, it was said, rendering any arrange- ment impossible by the violence of his demands—the tone of the British Government was far more subdued, and betrayed a wish to avoid a war with Russia at a time when we had been so near to one with Sweden, and when a reconciliation between the two powers had been found to be so unex- pectedly imminent.   Under these circumstances, though in 1717 Sir John Norris' annual expedition into the Baltic was heralded with big words, nothing came of it; the Swedes were not to be tempted from their harbours ; and the Russian quarrel was not fought out at sea.   The intolerable pressure exercised by the Russian troops in Mecklenburg induced the Imperial authorities, in defiance of Russia and, since Görtz was resuming his schemes, perhaps of Sweden also, to commission Hanover and Brunswick with the execution of the Empire against the refractory Duke of Mecklenburg-Schwerin, and an armed conflict actually took place, into the vicissitudes of which it is unnecessary to enter.   The subsequent withdrawal of the Russian troops from Mecklenburg, which has been so fre- quently attributed to the insistance of George I, was not really due to any action on his part, either as King or as Elector. It is rather to be explained as a concession to his French ally the Regent, with whom the Czar in August, 1717, concluded the treaty of Amsterdam, in which France promised to leave her subsidy treaty with Sweden unrenewed, in return for Russia's acceptance of French mediation in the matter of the Northern Peace.   In the ensuing years—1718 and 1719— the tension between Russia and Great Britain increased instead of relaxing ; and, delighted with the prospect of Russia, and possibly even Prussia, being brought into hostile relations with King George, the Jacobite agents in the Baltic

furnished more material than ever for Robethon to copy into
his papers[1]. In 1718 accordingly, so far as northern relations were concerned, the schemings of Görtz were resumed
with a better prospect of success than before, and peace
negotiations actually began in the Aland Islands under
Spanish mediation. Not only the acquisition of Bremen and
Verden, for which in the latter part of the year[2] we are not
surprised to find King George seeking to secure an imperial
guarantee, but British interests, the future of the Baltic trade,
and the question of the entire mastery of these waters, were
trembling in the balance. Yet what attention was likely in
these negotiations to be paid to the voice of Great Britain
who, though in truth already the foremost maritime power in
these regions, would become embroiled with both Russia and
Sweden for objects concerning her either remotely or not at
all? And should peace be concluded between the combatants—should that peace mean an alliance, and the plans of
Görtz and the calculations of Alberoni be realised—no consequence was more probable than the overthrow of the new
régime in Great Britain, and the driving backwards of the
course of our national history.

The death of Charles XII in December, 1718, necessarily
produced a complete change in the mutual relations of the
northern powers, and one which has to some extent obscured
the paradoxical situation of the period immediately preceding,
when Sweden and Russia were bidding for one another's
friendship, and Great Britain, chiefly in consequence of
Hanoverian action, was on almost equally bad terms with
both. In 1719, when the course of events in Southern
Europe was everywhere favourable to the interests of the
Quadruple Alliance and to the resolute policy of Stanhope,
a spirited endeavour was also made to follow out in the

---

[1] See vol. xi. of *Correspondence, passim.*

[2] November, *ib.* vol. xi. p. 163.

H

north a line of action consciously taken up by a responsible British statesmanship. The schemes of Görtz were at an end, and their author fell a victim to the audacity of his genius. For Sweden, reconstituted under Queen Ulrica Eleanora as an oligarchical government, the choice lay between a simple acceptance of Russian terms of peace, which would have at once reduced her to a position closely resembling vassalage towards the power of the Czar, and an adherence to the powers whose jealousy had been excited against his ascendancy in the Baltic—above all, to Great Britain. The personal inclinations of the Queen and of her consort, the hereditary Prince of Hesse-Cassel, who had worn the British uniform, and the wishes of a small but stedfast minority in the nobility, favoured the latter alternative. The British government, clearly recognising the danger of giving way to Russia in the Baltic, was disposed to seize the opportunity, which might pass away irrecoverably, for asserting its influence over Sweden, and secondarily over Denmark, and for bringing about such a final settlement of the northern quarrel as should preserve a fair balance among the Baltic states. Under these circumstances the British Cabinet resolved to send one of the ablest and most accomplished among the younger adherents of the ruling party, Lord Carteret, on a special embassy to Stockholm, to which Court the King, as Elector of Hanover, had already accredited a special envoy in the person of M. de Bassewitz [1]. The despatches and

---

[1] Henning Frederick von Bassewitz, who plays a prominent part in the *chronique scandaleuse* of the age, was another native of Mecklenburg, belonging by descent to its most ancient nobility. He was created a Count of the Holy Roman Empire for his services to the House of Austria. At St. Petersburg, where he had represented the Duke of Holstein-Gottorp, he was treated rather roughly by Peter the Great; and on his way to Stockholm he came into collision with Görtz. He was afterwards concerned in the transactions leading to Görtz's execution. (Cf. Vehse, *Die Höfe Mecklenburgs*, vol. i. pp. 222 seqq.)

letters of Carteret, written from the Swedish, and afterwards from the Danish, Court, fill four volumes of the extraordinarily ample collection of his papers in the British Museum [1]; and a volume in the Record Office, containing Stanhope's despatches from Hanover, with other correspondence belonging to the years 1719–20 [2], furnishes much supplementary information concerning the protracted negotiations conducted by Carteret at Stockholm and Copenhagen, by Polwarth at the latter Court, by Whitworth at Berlin, &c. Carteret is an egregious despatch-writer, free from diffuseness, notwithstanding the pleasure which he evidently takes in the process of literary composition, and, though possessed by an inborn love of the grand manner, quite capable of resorting on occasion to plainness of speech. The general course of his embassy cannot be narrated here [3]. In 1719 he made so successful a use of the presence of Sir John Norris' squadron in the Baltic as to induce the Swedish government, hampered though it was by the necessity of obtaining the concurrence of the Estates, to hold out against the Russian terms of peace and to conclude a preliminary treaty with Great Britain, which was confirmed after Sir John Norris had sailed up to Stockholm, and had thereby prevented the Russians from showing their faces at sea, and given Sweden breathing time for the winter. Early in 1720 a definitive defensive treaty was signed between Great Britain and Sweden against Russia and Denmark, limited, however, as against the latter, to the provision of subsidies only ; and about the same time, in accordance with our treaty of alliance with Prussia of August, 1719 [4], Great Britain and

---

[1] *Additional MSS.*, 22,511–22,514.

[2] *Regencies*, vol. xi., July 1, 1719 to February 20, 1720.

[3] An account of it will be found in Mr. Archibald Ballantyne's biography of Lord Carteret (1887).

[4] Frederick William I had consented to the treaty of alliance with Great Britain with the worst of grace, his antipathy being ineradicable

France with great difficulty mediated a treaty between Sweden
and Prussia, which was now by the cession of Stettin and certain other positions in Pomerania completely detached from
the Russian alliance.   Finally, towards Denmark Carteret,
who completed at Copenhagen the negotiations begun by
him from Stockholm, showed a firm hand, insisting upon the
retrocession of Stralsund and Rügen, with Wismar, to Sweden,
whose pride was thus salved, while France was flattered by
the adoption of her policy of leaving to Sweden a foothold
on German soil.   Denmark's compensation was limited to
her retaining the Duchy of Schleswig and receiving a sum
of money, which the coolness of the British negotiators
succeeded in reducing to a moderate figure.

The purposes of Stanhope and Carteret in these very
successful transactions of 1719 and 1720 had in so far been
fulfilled that, to quote an early despatch from the former urging
the Lords Justices to reinforce Sir John Norris's squadron
in the Baltic, the opportunity had been seized of 'awing the
Czar, saving Sweden,' and defeating Spain's last hope of
'forming a strong alliance against Great Britain in the north[1].'
The exertions of British diplomacy and the skilful demonstrations of the British fleet had therefore not been made in vain,
although we may be rather at a loss how to account for the
sentiment imported by Carteret into the struggle.   More than
once he employs the phraseology of the despatch in which he
reports the signature of the preliminary treaty with Sweden:
'I hope I have not exceeded the King's instructions. . . .

against his mother's family and nation.   His *marginalia* on the
despatches submitted to him on the occasion bear witness to these
sentiments.   'If I could see a few Hanoverian villages in flames,
I should feel quite well again. . . . Nothing but fraud can come from the
English; I hold with the Czar and Denmark.'   (Droysen, vol. iv. Part
II, pp. 216–7 and note.)   But he had yielded at last.

[1] *Record Office, Regencies*, vol. xi; Stanhope to Delahaye, July 1,
1719.

The Protestant cause will owe its preservation to him. This
—the Swedish—nation is poor and reduc'd at present, yet
their alliance is not to be scorned, but courted. . . . They
have as good swords and as good hearts as any in Europe [1].'
Our historical sympathy may be moved by this appeal; and
the particular adjective applied by Carteret to the cause of
a militarism which had overleapt itself must have touched
a responsive chord in many a British breast as well as in
that of King George I. But the interests of the British
nation were limited to keeping the Baltic open, which, as
we find Carteret very forcibly reminding the Danes, was far
more easily done without than with the predominance of
Russia in its waters; while King George's desire for a settlement with Sweden arose not from interest in her future, but
from a wish to secure the acquisition of Bremen and Verden.
Accordingly, the question of this acquisition dominated the
British as well as the Hanoverian negotiations at Stockholm,
and nothing could be more evident than that by the Swedes
the definitive cession of Bremen and Verden was regarded
as the *quid pro quo* for the protection of the British fleet.
Bassewitz had everything contingently in order by the time
of Carteret's arrival at Stockholm; and it was clearly understood on both sides that if Bremen and Verden were ceded
to Hanover, Great Britain would go the necessary lengths
in supporting Sweden against Russia [2]. In order, however,

---

[1] *British Museum Additional MSS.*, 22,511, p. 77.

[2] See *British Museum Additional MSS.*, 22,511, pp. 11-12.
Carteret writes to Stanhope, July 2, 1719, that he has 'brought the
Queen and her ministers to declare that they will make an absolute
cession, but upon such conditions as you must direct me upon.' 'I never
doubted,' he adds, putting into a dozen words the real nature of the
hazard run by Great Britain in attempting to settle simultaneously the
Baltic question and the cession of Bremen and Verden, 'but they would
part with these duchies, if King George would engage himself to do
more for them than they (the duchies) are worth.'

not only to spare the susceptibilities of the Swedes, but also to
prevent any sudden revocation on their part of the proposed
cession, Carteret had to use every possible ' management.'
He had to keep them ignorant of the desire of the British
Government to see the Swedish treaty with Prussia carried
through[1]. He had to defer to the feeling that Sweden must
not be driven altogether out of the Empire, on which she had
of old inflicted so much suffering in the cause of religion—
a feeling so strong as to make his good friend the Prince of
Hesse declare, that if he allowed this to happen he would be
coupé de tous les honnêtes gens. He had, to use a significant
phrase of his own, to treat 'with great neglect' the efforts of
Bernstorff and his Hanoverian colleagues to secure better terms
for Denmark than would have been permitted by the temper
of the Swedes, who hated the Danes almost worse than they
hated the Russians[2]; 'but, however, he' (Bernstorff) 'cannot
control anything of this nature[3].' With the aid of a patience
which must have found some relief in the communications
flowing from his facile pen, and of a courage never afraid
of assuming responsibility at a critical moment, Carteret
carried through so much of his task as fell within his sphere
of action, while at the same time enabling his Hanoverian
colleague to carry his special business to a conclusion. In
1720, Bremen and Verden were, as has been seen, definitively ceded by Sweden for a moderate money payment.
A very striking document in the Record Office, which I
have not seen quoted elsewhere, shows very clearly with
how correct a logic Swedish public opinion estimated the

[1] *British Museum Additional MSS.*, 22,511, p. 43, July 23 : ' Had
the Swedes suspected that King George interested himself in the satisfaction of the various members of the alliance against Sweden, they
would never have made so complete a cession of Bremen and Verden.'
And cf. *ib.*, p. 64.

[2] *Ib.*, pp. 160, 170 (October).   [3] *Ib.*, pp. 191–2

real nature of the transaction. The Emperor having with praiseworthy caution declined to grant to his good friend the Elector of Hanover and King of Great Britain investiture with the Duchy of Bremen and Principality of Verden, without formal proof that the cession had been approved by the constituted authorities of the kingdom of Sweden, Bassewitz was supplied with a resolution which had been passed for the purpose in the Senate at Stockholm. The protocol of this resolution runs as follows : ' We are indeed of opinion that the cession of Bremen, Verden, Stettin, and Pomerania [1] is a sensible loss to the kingdom, inasmuch as these conquests cost so much Swedish blood, were guaranteed by the Peace of Westphalia, &c., &c., but on comparing this loss with the harsh offers of the Czar, which he even desired to force upon us as a law, and this in an incendiary fashion [2], in order that he might thus become master of the Baltic Sea, &c., &c., we cannot but esteem as beneficial the engagements entered into with the King of Great Britain as such and as Elector of Hanover, together with his mediation and that of the French Crown with Russia, whereby we obtained resources with which to carry on the war and to secure a reasonable peace with the Czar, who of all our enemies is the most powerful [3].' In other words, the Swedes believed that by the cession of Bremen and Verden they had bought the friendship of Great Britain, which in 1719, when the Russian camp-fires were burning almost within sight of Stockholm, had saved that capital from a visit of the Russian fleet, and the Government from a complete surrender. But they knew only too well that the repeated appearances of the British

---

[1] Only part of Pomerania had been actually ceded to Prussia.

[2] This phrase seems to refer to the devastations of the Swedish coasts by which the Czar's peace overtures were accompanied in 1719 and 1720, and which were renewed in 1721.

[3] *Regencies*, vol. xii (Protocol of Swedish Senate. June 20, 1720).

admiral in these northern waters had not saved their coasts as far as Bothnia from being harried by the foe. Nor could they think it likely that in the peace, if ever it were concluded, the Czar would, in deference to the wishes of a Sovereign who had thwarted his designs and threatened his person, renounce Livonia, and with it the mastery of the Baltic.

Bremen and Verden were secured; but it was not with the aid of British mediation, proffered though this had been by Sir John Norris as it were at the sword's point, that the Swedish peace with Russia was at last concluded. Once more, in 1721, Sir John Norris appeared in the Baltic with a British fleet; but no results attended this concluding naval demonstration, and the belated scheme of a northern Quadruple Alliance put forward in this year proved still-born. Already in the latter part of the year 1720, when Carteret's Danish embassy was drawing to its close, and he was preparing for his return home by way of Hanover, the tone of his despatches shows that his hopes of obtaining satisfactory terms from the Czar were on the wane. As a matter of fact, the Peace of Nystad, concluded in September, 1721, left nothing to Sweden beyond Finland and part of Carelia, and Russia, as mistress of the whole of Livonia and of Revel, had become the dominant power in the Baltic. Sweden had not yet sunk permanently into a relation of dependance on Russia; but we shall see that Carteret's attempt in 1723 to revive the policy of 1719 broke down completely, and that at the time of the ill-judged war of 1741, which rendered Sweden's losses of territory permanent, we were on the friendliest of terms with her foe. The Bremen and Verden cession remained unrevoked, although as late as 1740 there had been some talk at Stockholm of an attempt to recover those territories [1].

[1] Had it been made, Great Britain would have been in the peculiar position of having by a subsidy-treaty 6,000 Hessian subjects of King

Not much difficulty will, I think, be felt at the present day in striking the balance between the advantages that accrued to Great Britain by this Hanoverian acquisition, and its inexpediency from the point of view of our national policy. All that can be said on the one side was urged by Townshend in reply to the protests of his Dutch correspondent Slingelandt, and was afterwards repeated with more argumentative force by Horace Walpole the elder [1]. But granting that the Hanoverian annexation implied access to what Townshend rather grandiloquently called 'the gates of the Empire,' and that it was unsatisfactory to leave these in the hands of Denmark—a Power that has come into collision with England both before and after the reign of George I— yet she could obviously have been kept out of Bremen and Verden by some other process than that of buying her out and coming close to the brink of war with Sweden. How serious a risk was thereby incurred for our northern interests was shown by the entire reversal of our Baltic policy so soon as on the death of Charles XII Russia had determined to overpower Sweden. But the latter Power, from whom payment had already been exacted, had no gratitude to spare for us; and thus the solution of the Baltic problem, which had so direct an interest for Great Britain, and in which an earlier and unprejudiced intervention might have enabled her to take a leading part, was accomplished without her and in her despite. The striking success of the negotiations carried on by Carteret and directed by Stanhope in 1719–20, should not blind us to the even more signal failure as a whole of the policy with which the most conspicuous of George I's Hanoverian successes is intertwined. The

Frederick I of Sweden (who had taken over the royal authority, such as it had become, from his Queen in 1720) to employ against a Swedish attack.

[1] Coxe, *Life of Sir Robert Walpole*, vol. i. pp. 160–1.

Personal Union, however, was itself to remain no stranger
to the consequences of this failure. It was in the name of
the freedom of Baltic commerce, but really to conciliate
the goodwill of Russia as the predominating Baltic Power,
that Hanover was in 1801 overrun by Russia on the bene-
volent suggestion of France.

The influence of Hanoverian statesmanship acts in no
specifically interested way in the wider range of transactions
to which I next proceed summarily to advert; but here, too,
it manifests itself in a measure unapproached in any later
period of the Personal Union. To judge of these transactions in their general connexion with our immediate
subject, it is necessary to go back for a moment. The
Peace of Nystad belongs already to a time when Great
Britain, strong in an alliance including both France and the
Empire, and victorious over the ambitious attempts of Spain,
aspired to become the arbitress of the affairs of the north.
Neither the conception nor the consummation of the policy
which had placed this country in so commanding a position
as that which it had reached towards the close of the second
decade of the century is to be ascribed, wholly or mainly,
to the inspiration of Hanoverian counsels ; just as it would
be delusive to seek the chief motive for the energy exhibited
by the statesmanship which carried out that policy in devotion to the interests of the new dynasty. Nevertheless, at
no other time during the continuance of the Union was the
conduct of our foreign affairs more immediately under the
eyes of the sovereign—especially when he was residing at
Hanover ; and at none was he in more constant communication and consultation with the politicians in possession
of his personal confidence, among whom Bernstorff, and
next to him Bothmer, were prominent. The great achievements of the foreign policy of George I's reign thus bear
the unmistakeable mark of the King's personal approval,

and of the co-operation of his Hanoverian counsellors. Townshend lost his hold upon the conduct of foreign affairs after the limits of his appreciation of dynastic purposes and methods had been made clear to the King by Sunderland, a master of this kind of exposition. The policy of the Triple and Quadruple Alliance, of which the chief credit rightly belongs to Stanhope, could not have been carried to so successful an issue except by a minister possessed, in the full sense of the term, of the confidence of the King, and in touch with his still most trusted advisers.

There can be no doubt but that the suggestion of an alliance between Great Britain and France, which constituted the basis of the new system of our foreign policy, was due neither to British nor to Hanoverian statesmen, but to the Regent Orleans himself. He was naturally anxious to protect his own future against the Spanish Bourbons, and was in particular desirous of preventing a good understanding between the Spanish and the British Governments, such as Alberoni was astutely seeking in the first instance to establish by means of commercial concessions, actual or pretended. The proposal of the British Cabinet to carry on at Paris negotiations for giving effect to the Regent's ideas had been rejected, largely it would seem because it was not wished to entrust them to Stair[1]. Thus the management of the business was in the first instance transferred to the Hague. This was still the diplomatic as the

---

[1] Stair was evidently much disliked at Paris (St. Simon attacks him with the utmost virulence), and was no fortunate choice as British Ambassador; but his innumerable letters in the *Robethon Correspondence* cannot be said to give the impression of a stiff, unbending disposition. He showed no ill-temper when the negotiation was taken out of his hands (*ib.*, vol. viii. p. 9). He repeatedly asked to be relieved of his ambassadorial functions on account of the inadequacy of his means.

neighbouring Amsterdam was the banking centre of Europe; but in the present instance the place was chosen in order that the Regent's personal intimate, the Abbé Dubois, with instructions, as Stanhope writes, 'full of sweetness, unction, and accommodation [1],' should meet the British minister there when *en route* for Hanover. Thither, as we saw, King George repaired in the summer of 1716, for as long a sojourn as could be made compatible with English public sentiment; and thither the continuation of the negotiations for the conclusion of the Anglo-French *entente* were accordingly transferred. Thus the peculiarity of the circumstances under which so extraordinary a result was so rapidly reached, by no means consists only in the choice of the French political agent (whom, by the way, George I seems to have afterwards befriended). Hanover was the locality where the *entente* was finally settled; and Hanoverian statesmanship took an active part in the proceedings that led to a result so little in accordance with English popular sentiment. At Hanover and Herrenhausen, in the forests surrounding the hunting-seat of the Göhrde, and in the peaceful avenues of Pyrmont, Stanhope and Bernstorff—or to put them in the order in which we find their names running off old Horace Walpole's pen [2], Bernstorff and Stanhope —enjoyed both far readier access to the ear of their common master, and more continuous opportunities for unsuspected consultation with one another, than they might have found, or cared to make use of, at St. James's. Thus by October, 1716, was concluded the so-called Triple Alliance, to which the assent of the United Provinces was with scant ceremony taken for granted; and by the following January it was actually signed. Its advantages to Great

---

[1] *Robethon Correspondence*, vol. viii. p. 32.
[2] *Ib.*, vol. viii. p. 107.

Britain were so closely connected with the increase of
security accruing from it to the Hanoverian dynasty that it
might well be regarded as a twofold triumph. The Regent,
in giving way about the Mardyke fortifications and re-
nouncing the shelter hitherto afforded to the Pretender in
France, had sacrificed positions persistently maintained by
Louis XIV as points of honour. And it must have enhanced
the satisfaction of George I and his Hanoverian ministers
to know that the Regent had arrived at so complete an
understanding in the teeth of Görtz's protestations at Paris
that Charles XII was more *piqué* against the King of Great
Britain than against any one else [1], and doubtless also of
insinuations that the Regent could not do better than take
up the cause of the Pretender. The completeness of the
success overwhelmed Townshend, who without impeding the
French negotiations had virtually stood aloof from them.
Sunderland prepared his fall, and Bothmer did his best to
make it easy [2]. The subsequent dismissal of Townshend
from the office to which he had consented to be transferred, completed, as you know, the declaration of the schism
in the Whig party. Stanhope now became First Lord of
the Treasury, and in 1718 one of the Secretaries of State,
Sunderland holding these offices in the inverse order; but
under either designation Stanhope was the actual head of
the Government. During his ascendancy the Hanoverian
influence was exercised more as a matter of course than
ever; nor was it till shortly before the close of his conduct
of affairs—and then apparently with his connivance [3]—that
this influence experienced a serious rebuff.

---

[1] Stair to Robethon, September 28, 1716 (*Robethon Correspondence*,
vol. viii. p. 116).

[2] *Robethon Correspondence*, vol. ix. p. 11.

[3] Lady Cowper's *Diary*, p. 145.

If in the Triple Alliance the interests of the dynasty had been very directly concerned, the Quadruple Alliance reflected one of its most cherished traditions. Which of these could compare with the devotion of the House of Brunswick Lüneburg to the House of Austria? This sentiment was as an article of faith with the Hanoverian advisers of George I, and it may reasonably be doubted whether without the patient and persevering labours of Bernstorff and Bothmer the politicians of the Vienna Hofburg would have given way even to the ardour of Stanhope. To Bothmer the Austrian alliance was, as he explicitly states, a matter of something more than an increase of military strength[1]; while in a letter rather hysterically urging the con-clusion of the alliance as an achievement certain to be of the greatest benefit to the human race, Dubois explicitly asserts that Bernstorff possesses more influence than anybody else with the Emperor[2]. The task which with their assistance was accomplished was the reverse of easy; for the Austrian acceptance of the proposed alliance was by no means only impeded by the Habsburg pride and prejudice which so vexed the souls of Sir Robert Walpole and his brother Horace; an equally real obstacle lay in the consideration that the secure establishment of the Regent Orleans in power in France implied the exclusion of Philip from the French throne, and that thus he and his line would remain in possession of the Spanish, to which the Emperor Charles had by no means renounced his pretensions. As late as January, 1718, the Regent was troubled by most serious apprehensions that the Emperor would after all prefer to treat directly with his Spanish rival[3].

We are fortunate enough to possess a document of some

[1] *Robethon Correspondence*, vol. ix. p. 2.
[2] *Ib.*, p. 282.
[3] *Ib.*, vol, viii. pp. 13, 21.

length, drawn up, as there can be no reason for doubting, by
the hand of Count Bothmer himself, which was designed
by him as a historical narrative of the negotiations for the
Quadruple Alliance in the years 1717 and 1718[1]. It was
not completed, or the conclusion, which contained an account
of the transactions at Madrid and the Hague, has been lost;
but it furnishes a consecutive account of the negotiations
upon which the establishment of the concert depended.
This narrative or memoir conclusively proves the importance
attached on the Austrian side, and more especially by the
extremely able Austrian negotiator Penteriedter, who plays
an important part in the diplomatic history of this period, to
the counsels of Bernstorff and Bothmer.   Furthermore, it
shows them to have acted on their own judgment, more like
independent allies than supplementary subordinates, in furthering the purposes of Stanhope as the leading representative
of British policy.   As is well known, Stanhope's project was
to bring about an amicable settlement between the Habsburg
Emperor and the Bourbon King of Spain, by the transfer to
the Emperor of Sicily in exchange for Sardinia, while the
succession in Parma and Tuscany was secured to Philip's
son, Don Carlos.   The disadvantages of the Emperor's position were augmented by his being still hampered by the
continuance of his Turkish war, although in August, 1717,
his arms were crowned by two brilliant victories.   Since the
aggressive attitude of Spain still remained unchecked, and
was still upheld by a strong party in the divided Council of
the Regent, and since the Emperor himself continued unwilling
to renounce all claim to the Spanish throne, it was a task of
no small difficulty to bring him into line with the policy
of the British and French governments.   But in 1718 (July)

[1] ' Memoiren des Grafen von Bothmer über die Quadrupelallianz,'
&c., published by Dr. R. Doebner in *Forschungen zur deutschen Geschichte*, xxvii. 2 (Göttingen, 1886).

peace was concluded between the Emperor and the Turks at
Passarowitz, under British mediation, prompted no doubt by
the interest of George I in what may be called the Eastern
Question[1].   The Emperor's course of action was finally

[1] Professor W. Michael, in his *Englische Geschichte*, &c., vol. i.
pp. 813–31, has directed attention to this episode of our diplomatic
history, hitherto scarcely noticed. Cardinal Alberoni had trusted to
alliances, conspiracies, and insurrections for sapping the strength of the
several members of the Quadruple Alliance; and among these
manœuvres there had been an attempt at forcing back the attention of the
House of Austria upon its own affairs by inducing Francis Rakoczi, the
hero of the great Hungarian insurrection of the first decade of the
century, to head one more rising against the Austrian dominion.   In
conjunction with this movement, the Turks had been instigated to
prosecute their war against the Emperor with renewed vigour.   It had
been actually in progress since 1716, having arisen out of the renewal of
hostilities between the Turks and their habitual adversary, the Signiory
of Venice.   In the course of this conflict, the Turks had recovered all
the conquests of Morosini, 'the last of the Venetians,' including the
Morea and Athens, which the Hanoverian soldiery had been instrumental
in helping to wrest out of their hands.   It seemed as if from the Dalma-
tian coast they might have continued their advance as far as the lagoons
which sheltered the discrowned Queen of the Adriatic.   In the event of
a Turkish attack upon Venice the Emperor was bound to render assistance to her by the treaty of Carlowitz, concluded in 1699 under the
mediation of Great Britain and the United Provinces—at a time when,
in apprehension of a speedy vacancy on the Spanish throne, William III
was above all anxious to put an end to a war which had pre-engaged
the military strength of the Empire.   In a sense the situation was not
very dissimilar in 1717 from that of 1699; but the military successes
gained by Prince Eugene in the month of August, 1717—the victory of
Peterwardein and the capture of Belgrade—surpassed in splendour those
of which part had fallen to his share during the former war.   The capture of Belgrade had in itself exercised an immediate and most notable
effect in the Emperor's favour in Italy[1]; and it had become difficult for the
mediating Powers to exert a restraining influence, more especially since
the claims of the victorious Prince Eugene upon the consideration of
Great Britain and the United Provinces were quite unparalleled.   Under
these circumstances the successful efforts of the diplomatic representa-

[1] St. Saphorin to Robethon; *Robethon Correspondence*, vol. ix. p. 220.

determined by the renewed violence of Spain, who, while plotting a northern league against the British throne, was preparing to settle affairs in the Mediterranean by a second *coup de main*, this time upon Sicily.   It is in the negotiations which preceded and helped to bring about this determination that we are able to follow step by step the action of the Hanoverian ministers.   Bernstorff and Bothmer were zealous in promoting the secret treaty by which the Emperor was guaranteed the support of Great Britain and France for the event of a resistance on the part of Spain to the proposed territorial arrangements in Italy.   Protracted discussions ensued as to possible modifications in

tives of these Powers, as to the selection of whom Bernstorff had been in active communication with the Grand Pensionary[1], seem entitled to particular recognition.

These were the envoys of the two Powers at Constantinople, the Dutchman Count Jacob Colyer, who had formerly taken part in the negotiations for the Peace of Carlowitz, and Edward Wortley Montagu, to whose sprightly consort we owe the first literary pictures of Turkish interiors.   The endeavours of these diplomatists to bring about a pacification between the Emperor and the Sultan had been carried on even before the fall of Belgrade; but when after that event peace conferences were actually opened at Passarowitz, Sir Robert Sutton had superseded Mr. Wortley Montagu.   What between the Imperial and Venetian plenipotentiaries and the Turkish, behind whom respectively stood in the background Prince Eugene and the new Grand Vizier Ibrahim, the Dutch and English diplomatists had need for infinite patience, and for not a little tact, before the conferences were brought to an effective conclusion.   Professor Wolfgang Michael points out that the Peace of Passarowitz from more points of view than one marks an epoch in the relations of Great Britain to the Eastern Question (as it used to be called), in which Austria seemed to be the Power destined to take the lion's share.   In so far, however, as the intervention of Great Britain was concerned, it manifestly continued the action of William III at Carlowitz, and must be looked upon as an effort, successful within its limits, to liberate the military strength of the House of Austria for co-operation in the policy of the Quadruple Alliance.

[1] *Robethon Correspondence*, vol. ix. p. 272.

I

these proposals, including the suggested reservation of Pisa and Leghorn as free cities under the protection of the Empire, and the garrisoning of certain places in Don Carlos' Italian territories by Spanish or even by British troops. That on such points as these considerable differences of opinion existed between Stanhope and the Hanoverian ministers, who were eager to do all in their power to strengthen the Emperor's position, is obvious from Bothmer's criticisms of the British statesman's conduct. The Austrian Penteriedter seems to have addressed himself directly to Bothmer and Bernstorff, as being sure to enter into his government's views of the situation, whereas Dubois only had recourse to it when exceptionally anxious to bring a personal influence to bear upon King George. The entire narration, so far as its author has carried it, opens a curious insight into the duplicated methods of British-Hanoverian diplomacy at this period, and exhibits Stanhope and the Hanoverian ministers as working side by side rather than on any definite plan of mutual combination[1].

Although, then, this famous treaty was signed in London (August 20, 1718), the earlier negotiations that were to lead to its conclusion had been carried on in Hanover. Nor is there perhaps any other important political transaction of the reign of which the responsibility, and we may unhesitatingly add the credit, distributes itself so unmistakeably between the chief British and Hanoverian statesmen concerned in it. Schaub was probably warranted in asserting that Dubois' most satisfactory contribution to the treaty was his insistance upon Stanhope being sent to Paris in order to

---

[1] Neither Schaub (afterwards Sir Luke Schaub) nor Robethon seems at this time to have been in Bothmer's good books; but I cannot here enter into illustrations or speculations. St. Saphorin (like Schaub, a Swiss by birth) did good service as our resident at Vienna in helping to carry through the scheme of the Quadruple Alliance in its final form.

carry it to a conclusion; for it would have been lost without
him [1]. But after all, the assent of the Regent to the principle
of the treaty was assured beforehand, and his resolution
merely needed strengthening against a factious minority in his
council. The *crux* lay in the difficulty of completing the
Emperor's conversion to the Western Alliance; and by
effecting this the Hanoverian statesman, whose anxiety for
the advantage and dignity of the Empire was unmistakeable,
materially contributed to the end in view.

The signature of the Austrian plenipotentiary had not yet
been appended to the treaty, and the Dutch had not yet
assented to it (indeed it took some six or seven months
more before their formal adhesion was brought about), when
it became known in London that the active resistance of
Spain, still under Alberoni's guidance, would still have to be
reckoned with. Failing this, the peace of Europe could not
yet be said to have been established on the basis, more solid
than that of the Utrecht treaties, upon which the parties
to the Quadruple Alliance had agreed. The events which
followed, and of which the cycle may be said to have closed
with the conclusion of the defensive alliance between Great
Britain, Spain and France, known as the Treaty of Madrid,
in 1721, were quite beyond the control of the influences at
present under discussion. On the assembling of the Congress of Cambray in the following year for the arrangement
of matters still left open between Spain and the Emperor,
the beginnings of fresh difficulties revealed themselves.
The history of these, and of the action of British policy
towards them, belongs, however, to a different chapter in
the history of the reign of George I, and at an early stage
in this new period the influence of Bernstorff, and so far as
I can see that of Bothmer, finally passed away. But in

[1] *Robethon Correspondence*, vol. x. p. 99 (Schaub to Robethon, July
17. 1718).

the great political achievements of reconciling France, and
more especially Austria, and of defeating Spain, Hanoverian
statesmanship may claim a large and honourable share.
The opposition offered to the conjunction between Stanhope
and the Hanoverian interest—a conjunction resting on no
merely personal basis—by Walpole and the 'disgusted'
section of the Whigs, was neither concealed nor scrupulous ;
but it cannot be credited with any profoundly patriotic motive,
and of a certainty it pursued no broadly national end.

In the above, I have noted at least the chief instances in
which what may fairly be called a dynastic policy is traceable
in the earlier half of the reign of George I.   This policy he
had as Elector inherited from his father and uncle before
him, and as they had accommodated it to the great designs
of William III, so during the war of the Spanish Succession
he had made it serviceable to the Grand Alliance, in whose
hands its founder had left the execution of his still uncompleted task.   The Bothmers and the Bernstorffs, though
assured by long habit of the personal confidence of their
prince, had, after exercising an unavoidable control over the
shifting of the scenes, been left in possession of an influence
more or less uncertain and intermittent, and occasionally
indebted to the aid of capricious or corrupt agencies, but
capable from time to time of unmistakeably and effectively
asserting itself.   On the other hand, neither Townshend,
whose ample correspondence nowhere so far as I have
observed belies the general impression of straightforwardness
conveyed by his public conduct, nor Stanhope, whose spirit
was far too high to allow us to suspect him of servility, was
consciously prepared to adapt his political action to an
extraneous pattern, or to allow the interests of the Electorate
to contribute otherwise than quite incidentally towards
deciding the action of the British Government.   But the fact
of the Personal Union existed, and with it a belief on the part

of the King that what concerned one of the states under his
rule concerned the other. Ranke has quoted a passage from
a letter from Sunderland to Townshend concerning the necessity of pressing on the conclusion of the Triple Alliance,
which is well worth reading with its context in the Townshend
papers [1]. For, together, they illustrate a point of view which
as yet neither English nor Hanoverian statesmen openly
took, but which a change in the situation of the affairs of
Europe—above all the occurrence of any serious peril to the
safety of the Electorate—might at any time oblige Great
Britain either decisively to accept or peremptorily to reject.
The King, Sunderland says, is 'very much surpris'd at the
strange notion that seems at present to prevail, as if the Parliament was not to concern themselves in anything that happens
in these parts of the world,' i.e. Germany or the Continent, and
looks upon it '*not onely as exposing him to all kind of affronts
but even to ruine*; and indeed this notion is nothing but the
old Tory one, that *England can subsist by itself, whatever
becomes of the rest of Europe, which has been so justly exploded
by the Wigs, ever since the Revolution.*' In this letter neither
the King's conception, nor the view which he reprobated,
can be said to be very clearly put; the meaning however is
obvious. Now, under the Hanoverian *régime*, as of old in the
days of the Grand Alliance, England's responsibilities are
not limited to the protection of her own safety and to the
advancement of her own interests, but extend to obligations
into which she has entered as to the safety and interests of
other States, among which from the nature of the case the
Electorate, with which she is united through the person of
their common sovereign, must stand first and foremost.
Had this conception of a British policy, including as an
integral part of it the defence of Hanover, been actually

[1] Historical MSS. Commission, Eleventh Report, Appendix IV,
p. 103.

adopted by responsible British statesmanship, a stage in the history of the Personal Union would have been reached beyond that with which we have occupied ourselves in the present lecture. But under no circumstances was British political action less likely to be swayed by the principle urged by George I, than during the ascendancy of Walpole, with whose advent to power the first or, as it may be called, the Bernstorff-Bothmer period of the Personal Union came, though not abruptly, to an end.

LECTURE IV

THE FOREIGN POLICY OF GEORGE I AND II
(1721–42)

OF the two veterans of Hanoverian state-craft mentioned
so frequently in our last lecture, Bernstorff had not
yet entirely relinquished public business for the cultivation of
fruit-trees, and Bothmer was still occasionally making use
of his official position for political purposes, when, in the
midst of the terrors of an unprecedented financial catastrophe,
the popular voice called Walpole to power. The ways of
thought and speech of this great national statesman were
wholly English, his training was quite undiplomatic, and he
never made any secret, either of his personal aversion to
members of the Hanoverian *junta*, or of his profound distrust
of the House of Austria, on their attachment to which their
political system hinged.   Townshend, whose loyalty to the
policy of the Triple Alliance had been unjustly impugned,
but whose dismissal from office had excluded him from any
share in the subsequent developement of that policy, succeeded to one of the vacant Secretaryships of State ; and to
the other—the Southern, not therefore that concerned with
the affairs of the countries in which he had gained his early
diplomatic laurels—Carteret was appointed.   Walpole can
hardly have been embarrassed by much wealth of choice
when he made this selection ; but nothing could be more
absurd than to suppose that, in making it, he had any wish

to gratify dynastic preferences or predilections[1].   During his
Northern mission Carteret had indeed entered very warmly
into the royal antipathy against the Czar; but he had shown
no interest in the specially Hanoverian aspects of the Northern
question, and in more than one instance had treated Hanoverian diplomacy and its agents with unconcealed disdain.
On the other hand, the strong autocratic vein in his disposition, which together with his fondness for rotundity of expression led him to lecture his colleagues as well as his opponents
when he had his pen in hand, and to give the rein to his wit
after dinner, sufficed to render it unlikely that his association
with Walpole would be enduring.   In the first instance, he had
to carry through the policy of Stanhope and bring Spain to the
conclusion of peace, but without the surrender of Gibraltar,
of which Stanhope had formerly held out a prospect.   This
he speedily effected (June 1721); and his perfect understanding with Dubois enabled them, by means of a joint
Anglo-French guarantee of the territories of both Spain and
Austria, to induce both these Powers to enter the Congress
of Cambray (1722).

So far Carteret had in harmony with Townshend carried
out a policy consistent with the general purposes of the
British Government and with its engagements.   But when
in 1723 both the Secretaries of State found themselves at
Hanover with King George I, the first occasion arose of
a difference between Carteret and his colleague in which the
former had the sympathy of the King.   The Peace of

[1] To a later date of course belongs Speaker Onslow's statement (see
the *Onslow Papers* in the Twelfth Report of the Historical MSS. Com-
mission, Appendix IX, pp. 471-2) that Walpole feared the influence which
Carteret had created for himself at Court largely by means of his intimacy
with the Hanoverian ministers (none of whom ever loved Walpole).
Possibly Carteret had begun to enter into closer relations with the
Hanoverians, when returning home in 1720 from Copenhagen by way of
Hanover.

Nystad was already bearing its fruits, and the Czar Peter was contemplating an armed intervention intended to over-awe the Swedish estates into settling the succession to the throne in such a way as ultimately to subject Sweden to Russian control[1]. Under these circumstances Carteret pro-posed at once to mobilise an English squadron for action in the Baltic. But the opportunity had in truth passed for confronting Russia on behalf of a broken Power like Sweden, and King George I reluctantly assented to the virtual inaction recommended by Townshend. The Swedish aristocracy bowed to the wishes of the Czar, to whose policy it remained obsequious during the whole period of the ascendancy of the Hats (to 1738). Indeed when in 1726 (shortly before the death of the Empress Catharine I) a British fleet anchored in the roads of Revel, its object was to prevent a joint Russo-Swedish attack upon Denmark, which might have resulted in the restoration of part of the Duchy of Schleswig to the House of Holstein-Gottorp. In the unhappy war of 1741, when Sweden's impotent attempt to regain her former boundaries ended in the disastrous Peace of Åbo (1743), she stood alone, and the succession was secured to the House of Holstein-Gottorp, notwithstanding the threat of a Danish in-tervention in which George II intended to have participated as Elector of Hanover[2]. But Great Britain was then in close alliance with Russia, and Sweden's part seemed to have been finally played out among the leading Powers of the North.

---

[1] By naming as successor the Duke (Charles Frederick) of Hol-stein-Gottorp, who was a suitor for the hand of the Czar's daughter Anna.

[2] A Holstein-Gottorp prince, though not the son of Russia's original candidate, actually succeeded Frederick I in 1750. In 1743 the Danes were promised the succession of their Crown-Prince in return for an alliance with Sweden, and the rumour of this arrangement is thought to have mitigated in some degree the rigour of the conditions imposed by the Russians at Åbo.

Mr. John Morley[1], in his brief chapter on the foreign
policy of Walpole's administration, has in all probability
correctly gauged the significance of this occasion, the first
on which Carteret pressed a 'spirited' line of conduct upon
a sovereign whose willingness to engage in it was restrained
by his other advisers.   Walpole's policy—and Townshend's,
while they acted together—was not and could not be a policy
of peace at any price, least of all at the price of the security
of the throne to which his perception of the best interests of
his country made him so loyal a servant.   But he wished
Great Britain to keep free from all engagements which it
was possible for her to avoid ; and he would not hear of her
rushing into a belated war with the Czar for a cause—the
preservation of a balance of power in the Baltic—which had
to all intents and purposes been already sacrificed at Nystad.
On the other hand, both he and his much-abused brother
Horace (who, though gifted with few of the arts and
graces of the diplomatic profession, often penetrated to the
root of the matter in his state-papers and letters) clearly
recognised the advantage of permanently strengthening our
position in the North, which was of so high an importance to
our commercial interests, by an alliance with Prussia.   It was
fortunate that the jealousy inspired by the aggressive policy
of the Czar acted as a counterpoise to the personal feelings
of King George I ; or the celebrated double-marriage project
which was to play so conspicuous a part in the family history
of the dynasty in the earlier years of the ensuing reign
could hardly have been already at this time on the *tapis*.
But for the present the transactions between the two houses
were confined to less delicate ground, and a step of considerable importance was gained by the Treaty of Charlottenburg
between Great Britain and Prussia (October 1723) which

[1] Walpole, *English Statesman Series* (1889), p. 203.

renewed the defensive alliance of 1690, and extended it to the German territories of the British Sovereign.

Before, however, Walpole had to meet a problem of greater difficulty for British statesmanship and requiring a solution directly opposed to the traditions of Hanoverian policy, Carteret's connexion with the conduct of foreign affairs had ceased. He had, while at Hanover, sought to strengthen his influence with the Countess of Darlington and the Countess of Platen by entering into their design of making a brilliant French marriage for a young lady born for greatness as the niece of the former and daughter of the latter favourite. Her intended husband, the Count St. Florentin, was the son of the Marquis La Vrillière, Secretary of State under the Regent and Dubois; and it was part of the scheme to give *éclat* to the match by securing from the Regent a dukedom for the head of the family which was to become allied to King George I's mistresses. This not in itself very baleful intrigue, in the success of which the King unluckily took a very particular personal interest, may be said to have rent the Foreign Office in twain. It was actively carried on at Paris by Sir Luke Schaub, the adventurous diplomatic agent who had transferred his official allegiance from Stanhope to Carteret, while at a little distance Bolingbroke cast an urbane shadow over the transaction as of one who an' he would could do much to expedite its course. Bernstorff, whose flickering influence in affairs of State might have been fanned into new life by the success of the project, and Bothmer, who came over from London to Hanover to lend his advice, were concerned in the business. Unfortunately Carteret, who must have thought the opportunity of rendering a personal service in such a quarter too good to lose, overreached himself in trying to take advantage of it. The history of the failure of the dukedom scheme may be read in the pages of St. Simon: it had become inevitable after the death of Dubois had been followed by that of the Regent; and it led not only to the recall of Schaub, and the establishment as ambassador at Paris of Horace Walpole, who had been sent over by his brother to watch the course of affairs, but also to the transfer of Carteret himself from his Secretaryship of State to the Lord Lieutenancy of Ireland (1724). It seems further to have brought about Bernstorff's withdrawal from the Privy Council at Hanover, where his place was in 1723 taken by a Hardenberg[1]. His day was past, and though Bothmer still remained to represent the traditions of the earlier part of the reign, they must have lost much of their force, more especially as the Duchess of Kendal had never shown herself more inclined to support Walpole[2]. Undoubtedly jealousies within the British cabinet, as well as a rivalry of another sort, must be included among both the causes and the consequences of a design upon the success of which Carteret had with even more than his usual rashness reckoned; but it seems futile to ascribe to Walpole's—or for that matter, to Townshend's—personal fears of Carteret's ascendancy their opposition to what began and ended as an unworthy intrigue.

The question however arises whether, had Carteret continued in office, so determined a resistance would have been made by the British Government to the action of the Power to which the Hanoverian dynasty was bound by the closest of traditional ties, and of whose alliance Carteret was in later days to stand forth as the most effective supporter. For it was now that the first rift was made in a political friendship of long standing and great solidity, though of course it had its real root, not in any British enthusiasm

---

[1] C. U. von Hardenberg, who became *Kammerpräsident*.
[2] Her later dealings with Bolingbroke do not concern us here.

for the Austrian claims to the Spanish throne, but in the British belief in the conservative character of the Imperial policy. During nearly two generations the alliance of the House of Austria had seemed an indispensable element in the policy which William III had handed down to the Whigs, and which had derived a fresh sanction from the loyal adherence to that House of the Hanoverian dynasty. The events, however, which ensued upon the meeting of the Congress of Cambray demonstrated the untrustworthiness of this time-honoured alliance, at all events, to the eyes of the brothers Walpole, nor could they fail to become all the more sceptical of its value, since Great Britain was at this very time entering into closer relations with Prussia, whose position had been so much strengthened both in Northern Europe and in the Empire by the results of the Northern War.

Whatever may be thought as to the unwillingness of the Emperor Charles VI to give way to the Maritime Powers on the subject of his East India Company, it seems clear that this formed the original impediment to a satisfactory issue of the Congress of Cambray which a Franco-Spanish quarrel actually broke up in 1725. Spain having now resolved to settle her differences with the Emperor at first hand, and having naturally taken deep umbrage at the brusque dismissal of the Infanta from France as a preliminary to the marriage of Louis XV to Maria Lescynska, Ripperda was able to press the so-called First Treaty of Vienna to a conclusion. The real gain of the agreement, however, accrued not to Spain, who most assuredly could through the Quadruple Alliance have secured the desired Imperial concessions as to the future dominions of Don Carlos, but to the Emperor, who found in the Spanish recognition of the Pragmatic Sanction his best equivalent for his abandonment of his Western allies. With these dynastic advantages secured, the historic ally of

Great Britain was not less ready than was the prince whose claims to the Spanish throne she had so persistently aided him in opposing, to play fast and loose with the question of the settlement of her own throne and government, by contemplating engagements as to an eventual support of the Pretender[1]. Thus, not only were the European relations which it had been the purpose of the Quadruple Alliance to guarantee, fundamentally disturbed; but the system of government established in Great Britain as the termination of a long-protracted era of civil troubles was, together with the endurance of the Hanoverian dynasty, to be thrown into the melting-pot of the general conflict.

The Treaty of Hanover between Great Britain, France, and Prussia (September 1725), which was designed as a direct retort to the First Treaty of Vienna, is therefore, notwithstanding its name, in no sense to be regarded as dictated by purely or mainly dynastic motives. The main responsibility of this agreement, which obviously diverts the course of our policy from the direction which it had previously pursued under Stanhope and was afterwards to resume under Carteret, rests with Townshend. But Walpole, who had only hesitatingly agreed to the Treaty of Hanover as an inevitable measure of self-defence, was found ready to follow it up by the requisite extended action. With the sturdiness

---

[1] I do not believe that any *actual* undertaking for the support of the Pretender was ever entered into by Charles VI, though this was asserted in the King's speech of 1727 referred to below. But as early as February 16, 1726, Horace Walpole asserted in Parliament that 'the imperial ministry at Vienna did not scruple to insinuate that if the King persisted in his resolution to take measures in opposition to the treaty of Vienna, the Emperor would not only think himself disengaged from the guaranty of the Protestant succession to the crown of Great Britain, but that such conduct might be attended with serious consequences to His Majesty's dominions in Germany.' (Coxe, *Life of Lord Walpole*, vol. i. p. 200.) Can it be doubted that he was near the mark?

which helps to account for his long-enduring Parliamentary ascendancy he bore the brunt of the Opposition clamour which absurdly denounced the treaty as subservient to Hanoverian interests.   As a matter of fact it had been concluded against the instincts of King George I and his Hanoverian advisers, apprehensive lest the Electorate might suffer from the wrath of the Emperor, as a party to the Treaty of Vienna. How could they be expected to approve the clause by which the Kings of Great Britain and Prussia agreed, in the event of a declaration of war by the Emperor against France, to abstain from furnishing their contingents to him as princes of the Empire, unless they deemed themselves unable to dispense with doing so—a somewhat inept way of expressing their intention of being guided by circumstances as to keeping or making their engagements.   And in the case of King George I a further gloss was put upon the compact by the subsidy-treaty concluded by him in March, 1726, with the Landgrave Charles of Hesse-Cassel [1], by which this prince of the Empire undertook to furnish his fellow-prince on the British throne with a force of 12,000 men; as well as by the subsequent treaty of November, 1727, with the Duke of Brunswick-Wolfenbüttel for a force of 5000.   In 1728 these treaties were violently attacked in Parliament as designed for the benefit of Hanover.   Undoubtedly the possible consequences of the Treaty of Hanover were present to the King's mind, and it was to meet them that the subsidy-treaties were concluded; yet it is curious that the Elector should have so materially weakened the defence of the Empire, besides consenting to make so light of his direct obligations towards it [2].

[1] The father of King Frederick I of Sweden, who succeeded as Landgrave in 1730.

[2] From the English point of view it must however be repeated that if the country was not to be left unprepared for war—a responsibility

For some time the political situation defined by the First
Treaty of Vienna and its secret articles, and by the counter-
treaty of Hanover, from which however (as we shall see
below) Prussia allowed herself to be gradually detached,
remained ominous of a general European conflict.   British
policy had to content itself with adhering steadily to the
principles of the Quadruple Alliance, abandoned for the
time by Austria in favour of a separate understanding with
Spain.   In these troubled years, when the House of Hanover
had subordinated its traditional preferences to the demands
of a situation full of peril to its own tenure of the British
throne, we shall not expect to find many traces of Hanoverian
opposition to the unsympathetic policy of Walpole and
Townshend.   Carteret had been succeeded in his Secretaryship of State by the Duke of Newcastle, from whom no
combinations in foreign affairs conflicting with their own were
to be apprehended by the leading ministers[1]; and at Paris

which Walpole was as unwilling to incur as Stanhope had been before
him—it is difficult to see how the requisite troops could have been
supplied unless by subsidy-treaties.   England could not supplement the
mercenary system like Prussia by recruiting from her neighbours' territories ; and a national militia, as we afterwards found, was not to be
stamped out of the earth.   Whether the subsidy-treaties were economi-
cally managed is a different question.   The Brunswick-Wolfenbüttel
treaty for £25,000 per annum seems in about half-a-dozen years to have
cost the country nearly ten times that sum.   See *Calendar of Treasury
Papers*, 1731–4, p. 97.

[1] At the close of his long political career—when nearly heart-broken by
not being invited to carry it on a little further—Newcastle philosophised
with some reason (though with scant power of expression) on the
' neglect of foreign affairs ' which he had observed in the British statesmen of his day, not excepting even Chatham, ' who raised himself and
his reputation by a contrary conduct.'   But the ' application ' with
which he concludes is typical.   ' I don't pretend to say what, or with
whom those alliances should be made ; that must depend upon circumstances, and the condition and disposition of the respective Powers; but
I mean all such connexions to be formed upon the principle of pre-

Walpole's brother Horace had dexterously contrived to secure the personal confidence of Fleury, who from 1726 onwards enjoyed a tenure of ministerial power comparable in length and steadiness to Walpole's own, but who like him in the end drifted against his own judgment into war.

It was however, and continues to be, asserted that the intrigues of Baron Palm, the Imperial Resident at the Court of St. James', carried on in this period of estrangement between the British and Imperial Governments, were fostered by the Duchess of Kendal and the Hanoverian ministers. As to Baron Palm's excess of zeal there can be no manner of doubt. It has not I think been noticed elsewhere that in the summer of 1718—when the negotiations for the Quadruple Alliance were in progress—Palm was regarded as an unsatisfactory representative of the Imperial Government in London[1]. How far, however, his precipitancy was the cause of the collision which at the very close of George I's reign nearly led to the outbreak of the general war which both Walpole and Fleury had laboured so sedulously to postpone—or whether Hanoverian cabals actually inclined Walpole and Townshend to an attempt to force the situation at home—it is not very easy to determine. At the same time, the estimate of Walpole's character which commends itself to my judgment, leads me unhesitatingly to reject any suggestion that he endeavoured to hasten a general war because in the closing months of the reign he had reason to fear for his tenure of power.

serving the peace, as Sir Robert Walpole, that enemy of foreign connexions, always said, *Preventive and Defensive.*' (Newcastle to Rockingham, July 8, 1767, in *Changes in the Ministry*, 1765-7, edited for the Royal Historical Society by Miss Mary Bateson, 1898.)

[1] Schaub writing to Robethon on July 21 (*Robethon Correspondence*, vol. x. p. 103), while recommending that St. Saphorin should remain as Resident at Vienna, states the latter to be strongly of opinion that Palm should be moved from London to some other post.

Whatever part may have been played by the Duchess of Kendal in urging the views of the Imperial Court may be safely attributed to her habitual willingness, in return for a direct consideration, to set a manœuvre in motion and then leave it to take its course. In any case, if George I and Bothmer were by Palm's action rendered more reluctant than ever to resist the Court of Vienna, and more alive than before to the dangers for the Electorate involved in the Treaty of Hanover, the British ministry were by it driven forward to the brink of extreme measures. In January, 1727, the King's speech declared, and founded a demand of readiness for war upon the declaration, that a secret agreement had been concluded between the Allies of Vienna for placing the Pretender on the British throne. Palm was hereupon instructed to tender to the King a memorial protesting in no measured terms against this charge as fictitious, and directed, in an angry letter from the Imperial Chancellor Count Zinzendorff, to publish the document. Instead of delaying a procedure so utterly irregular, he so to speak rushed his *ultimatum*, and promptly received his passports[1]. The British Resident at Vienna having been likewise dismissed, and the Spanish minister at St. James' having previously taken his departure, war with both Powers seemed inevitable.

Spain, however, was after all at the last moment left in the lurch by her ally, and her offensive effort broke harmless on the Rock of Gibraltar. The league of the Western was joined by the Scandinavian Powers, Prussia remaining neutral; and the Emperor, agreeing to a compromise about his Ostend Company, and abandoning any further attempt to settle matters for himself with Spain, left over a general settlement to another European Congress. Thus the reign of George I ended with the successful assertion of the policy of Walpole

[1] Baron Palm reappears in Germany as a combative diplomatist in 1744. (See Droysen, vol. v. part ii. p. 193.)

and Townshend against the attempt to override that policy
made by a Power whom a traditional attachment rendered it
difficult for the House of Hanover to resist, more especially
when it was influenced in the same direction by apprehensions
largely founded on the expected support of Austria by Russia
in the event of the outbreak of war.   George I is supposed
to have towards the close of his reign become weary of
Walpole, which is quite possible.   But nothing is less likely
than that the sagacious King had any intention of emancipating
himself from the guidance of his great minister either at home
or abroad.   The emotions of the English people, so easily
stirred when the hand of death touches kings and queens in
their turn, remained quiescent at the tidings of our first
Hanoverian Sovereign's sudden decease on his last journey
to his German home.   But he had not been unfaithful to
the spirit of the settlement to which he owed his royal
throne ; and the longer he had reigned, the more fully
had his policy met the responsibilities, which in reason
he knew to be paramount, of his position as a British
Sovereign.

With the accession of King George II it might have
seemed as if the inconveniences and disadvantages of the
Personal Union, even if they were not altogether removed,
were at least likely to be materially diminished.   So long as
the old King lived, his son and heir was, according to the
testimony of Lord Hervey, universally supposed to love
England and hate Germany [1].   What is more to the purpose,
George II, whose self-confidence was greater than his father's,
and who no doubt also cherished a more ardent ambition,
had from a relatively early age familiarised himself with the
idea of British rule.   And although he was late in arriving
at a perception of the distance which separated the ideals of

[1] *Memoirs*, vol. ii. p. 201.

a personal monarchy from the principles of British constitutional government, in the earlier part of his reign he had
by his side, in the person of Queen Caroline, an adviser at
once thoroughly devoted to the interests of his dynasty, and
capable of pursuing them in a spirit in which there was but
little pettiness and barely a thought of self. Nor, in esti-
mating the causes of his long-enduring unpopularity, should
it be overlooked that he had after all not himself chosen the
position in which he was placed by his twofold sovereignty
and of which, by the obstinacy of his behaviour and the
brusquerie of his manner, he did his utmost to emphasise the
unreasonableness. There is something humiliating in the
mass of reproach, satire, and insult which George II drew
down upon himself by his repeated and prolonged absences
at Hanover, from the withering sneers of Pope to the coarse
pasquinades stuck up at the corners of the London streets
and on the very gates of St. James' Palace[1]; but though
these visits were largely, they were not wholly prompted or
protracted by the desire of self-indulgence, and the volume
of parliamentary and popular obloquy which they provoked
was really out of proportion to its cause. He learnt his
lesson neither at once nor easily; and even after he had
virtually yielded to a Parliament which he could not control,
and a people whose loyalty he had failed to attract, he showed
himself no adept in the last art of Kings—that of graciously
yielding to a will other than their own. But though in the
successive periods of his reign hardly a mood of obstinacy,
hardly a movement of *pique* seems to be left unchronicled
by the most minute and malicious of observers, yet
the fact remains that neither obstinacy of opinion, nor
vehemence of resentment, nor absorbing selfishness of aim,
prevented him in the last resort from responding to the

[1] Hervey, ii. 362.

demands of the great national epoch in which he was called
upon to play his part[1].

I pass over, as calling for little or no comment from our
point of view, the earliest portion of George II's reign, which
may be taken as covering the period when, with the assistance
of Queen Caroline, Walpole was in practically undisturbed
control of affairs. Most assuredly the Queen merited the
recognition which has been freely accorded to her for enabling
Walpole during these years to maintain a policy of peace
against contrary influences, of which the King's personality was the main source. The Secretaries of State during

---

[1] It might be worth the while of some biographical historian with
space at his command, to analyse more carefully the singularly strong
odium which King George II excited against himself, and not only in
those to whom he was only known at a distance. Thus, for instance,
Lord Hervey as a politician thought with Walpole, and detested the
Hanoverian and German influences to which he repeatedly described the
King as subject. But in such a passage as that in *Memoirs*, vol. ii.
p. 35, he seems to imply that the bellicose attitude assumed by
George II in reference to the national policy should in sum be set down
to personal rather than to 'German' motives. It was certainly unlucky
that a military ambition, which would have been held highly creditable
in a Prince of Brunswick-Wolfenbüttel, should have seemed a foible in
the King of Great Britain; that it should have been impregnated with
jealousy by his cognisance of his Prussian brother-in-law's superior
opportunities in the way of recruiting; that he should have had to keep
up the numbers of his army not only in the teeth of his Parliament but
against the wishes of the minister by whom he managed the process
(*ib.*, p. 230); and that when at last he stood before his contemporaries
as the successor of Marlborough, a single day of victory should have
exhausted his assumption of the character. On the other hand, his
devotion to the interests of the Empire was genuine, and was all the
stronger because it was thoroughly shared by Queen Caroline. Her at
least Lord Hervey understood to perfection, nor can he be supposed to
have intended to speak anything but the truth when (*ib.*, p. 37) he goes
out of his way to assert that, 'wherever the interests of Germany and
the honour of the Empire were concerned, her thoughts and reasonings
were often as German and Imperial as if England had been out of the
question'; with more to the same purpose.

these years were, until 1730, Townshend and Newcastle;
but after the tension between the former and Walpole had
at last ended in an open rupture, his place was taken by
Harrington, the William Stanhope whose Spanish experience
had confirmed in him a reticent dignity of bearing to which
the irretentiveness of his fellow Secretary must have stood
in odd contrast. Notwithstanding the abuse poured on
Harrington by Hervey, he must have been a statesman of
some tact and judgment, and it is to his credit that he should
gradually have conquered the good will of both the King and
Walpole, which had at first been withheld from him for no
faults of his own [1]. The task of the British foreign ministers
of this period was in any case one requiring a patience such
as had not been distinctive of the bearing of Carteret. Before
the impression created by the Emperor's compromising
advances to Spain could be altogether effaced, there was
some vacillation on his part, and much persistency was
needed on that of the British Government. When after
prolonged discussions Spain at last (November, 1729) assented
to the Treaty of Seville, the Emperor held aloof from the
settlement, deeply offended by the provision substituting
Spanish for neutral garrisons in certain important places in the
Italian duchies destined for Don Carlos, over which the Empire
still claimed a feudal overlordship. In risking an armed
collision with the Emperor [2] the Government of King George I
certainly ignored Hanoverian traditions; and its determination might seem to have met with an appropriate reward in
the acceptance of the Seville Treaty by the Emperor in the
Second Treaty of Vienna (March, 1731). But the concession

[1] See Stanhope, vol. ii. p. 153. The King was prejudiced against
him on account of his brother Charles, Walpole by jealousy of his
kinsman, Lord Stanhope.
[2] Who on the death of the last Farnese early in 1731 actually
occupied Parma.

by which Great Britain had secured this adhesion—viz. the recognition of the Pragmatic Sanction—was one which, for her part, France was as yet by no means prepared to make. This unwillingness, and the tension which existed between herself and Spain, caused France to abstain from any participation in the new Vienna Treaty, which accordingly marks a weakening of the bond which for fourteen years had united her to Great Britain. The strongest link had indeed been taken away on the death of the Regent Orleans; but Walpole, from whom Townshend had before this at last separated, must be held responsible for Great Britain's precipitate guarantee of the Pragmatic Sanction. His foreign policy, though never wanting in intelligence, had the fatal defect of shaping itself all too readily to the exigencies of the moment—in general the parliamentary moment; and he had taken this step, in contravention of his habitual attitude towards the House of Habsburg, without consulting France or taking account of the sentiments of his own sovereign. But the historic French jealousy of the greatness of Austria was still far from extinct; and George II, as Elector of Hanover, could not but dislike any attempt to settle a question so deeply affecting the future of Germany in this anticipatory fashion. Thus the Second Treaty of Vienna marks not only the termination of an old series of contentions, but also the beginning of a new. Estranged from Austria, France drew nearer to Spain; and two years later, under the immediate influence of commercial jealousy of Great Britain, and of her determination to remain neutral in the War of the Polish Succession, the two Bourbon Courts concluded an agreement which may be regarded as the germ of their celebrated Family Compact[1]. On the other hand,—as if

[1] See Sir John Seeley's paper in the *English Historical Review* for January, 1886; though the conclusions there advanced perhaps in some respects overshot the mark.

a Nemesis had visited Walpole's rashness upon the country which it was the wish of his heart to keep out of war or engagements leading to war,—Great Britain once more entered into relations of intimacy with Austria that could not but momentously affect our position in the European conflict, should all the guarantees secured by Charles VI prove inadequate in the crisis.

Meanwhile, what was the nature of our relations with the Power which, when that time came, was to stand in the van of the assault upon the House of Habsburg, and which, when the long struggle was at last over, was to be found to have made good its claim to rank among the Great Powers of Europe? We have arrived at a chapter of British policy which, down almost to the dissolution of the Personal Union, invites a special consideration of certain motives of action influencing the Hanoverian dynasty and government as such, which in the latter part of George II's reign become of even greater significance than the traditional attachment of his line to the House of Austria.

The ancient jealousies between the Hanoverian and Prussian dynasties had, as has been seen, been from time to time assuaged by intermarriages, and suspended by the repeated necessity of agreeing on the protection of joint interests, more especially against the overbearing Baltic policy of Russia. So recurrent was the need of a defensive combination for this purpose that the following observation which, in 1747, old Horace Walpole had the courage to address to the Duke of Cumberland[1], might be applied to the condition of things during the greater part of the previous half-century. 'The necessity,' he wrote, ' of the friendship of Prussia, who with Sweden will keep the Czarina *en échec* and frighten Denmark, is so obvious that I wonder the Hanoverian

---

[1] See the second of his very noteworthy letters to the Duke in Coxe, *Life of Lord Walpole*, vol. ii. p. 210.

ministers have not employed their utmost dexterity and
credit, for the sake of their own country, to procure a perfect
good understanding between His Majesty and the King of
Prussia.' But the attempts periodically made to establish
such an agreement, whether or not dignified with the name
of Perpetual Alliances, were of their nature provisional; and
the project of the double marriage, on which I need not
expatiate to readers of Carlyle, dragged its way along with
very changeful chances of accomplishment. The design was
pressed on by the Queen of Prussia—George I's daughter
Sophia Dorothea—with pathetic persistency, whatever might
chance to be the aspect of the political horizon; and the
prosecution of it contributed to the estrangement of both
Frederick and his sister Wilhelmina from their father. It
ultimately broke down completely in consequence of the
reversal of Prussian policy of which we are about to speak;
and in 1730 the estrangement between Frederick William I
and his eldest son was, as you know, near ending in an awful
catastrophe. No love was lost between King George II and
his brother-in-law; each, as Lord Hervey puts it [1], thought
and spoke much the same of the other,—but we need not
repeat the unhoneyed epithets, nor discuss the evidence as to
the various personal motives in which rumour asserted the
root of all this ill-will to lie. What is certain is that two
questions of territorial politics served to interfuse with dynastic
jealousies the personal antipathies of the two Kings against
one another. One of these was the prolongation of the
Hanoverian occupation of Mecklenburg, on the plea that
though the execution with which the Elector was charged
had technically come to an end, its cost still needed to be
made good. The other sprang from the chaotic condition
of affairs in East Frisia, parts of which were under the control

[1] *Memoirs*, vol. iii. p. 349.

of the local estates, while over others the States-General of the United Provinces, as guarantors of certain compacts, claimed authority; and Brunswick, Brandenburg, and other troops had taken up positions in the country with a view to future contingencies. For the reversion of the principality of the Cirkzemas, which included a very desirable sea-board— the ' signiory of Embden' had been thought a rare prize in the Elisabethan age—was disputed by the Houses of Hanover and Brandenburg, the former claiming it on the strength of an ancestral treaty unconfirmed by Imperial authority, the latter by virtue of an Imperial grant. Considering the clear superiority of the Brandenburg claim, George II would have done well to attempt a compromise as to his own, and such a scheme was actually recommended by the Hanoverian Privy Council. But he was obstinate; the succession to this desirable territory was left unsettled, and when Charles Edzard, the last male scion of the Cirkzemas, died in 1744, the disputed inheritance was pocketed by Frederick II, with a promptitude peculiar to him [1]. A series of pettier, but highly irritating, occasions of friction was periodically supplied by the crimps whose business it was to find recruits for King Frederick William I's army, and more especially for his tall regiment of guards, and who constantly harried the Hanoverian territories bordering on his own, prolific, as they are to this day, of men of stature and stamina.

We saw how, towards the close of the reign of George I, Prussia had allowed herself to be detached from the Treaty of Hanover, having concluded with the Emperor the secret Treaty of Wusterhausen (November, 1726), in which she

---

[1] East Frisia, after successively undergoing annexation to the kingdom of Holland and to the French Empire, was in 1815 ceded by Prussia to the new kingdom of Hanover, and as part of this reverted once more to Prussia in 1866.

acknowledged the Pragmatic Sanction, and after which she even listened to insinuations as to the transfer to herself of Bremen and Verden in return for a renunciation of her claims upon the succession in the Rhenish duchy of Berg. The knowledge of this Austro-Prussian agreement had weighed with the Western Powers when endeavouring to thwart the Emperor's design of an independent settlement of his differences with Spain. Early in 1729, as has been seen, Walpole and Townshend were intent upon finding a solution which would bring Spain over to the side of peace, while war seemed imminent between France and Austria. It was at this season that King George II suddenly resolved to pay his first visit to Hanover since his accession to the British throne. He was called thither, as a royal message informed the Houses of Parliament, by divers reasons of importance; and the chief of these proved to be a secret treaty of alliance between the Emperor and Prussia, concluded at the close of the preceding year (December 23, 1728), by which the Wusterhausen agreement was converted into a permanent defensive alliance. Whether or not the two Powers might carry out the larger plan of settling in common their relations with Russia, it was clear that Prussia had thrown herself unreservedly into the Emperor's arms, no doubt strongly actuated by the belief that his authority would now settle in her favour her various outstanding controversies with Hanover. Townshend was so exasperated that he would unhesitatingly have risked a rupture with Austria, but Walpole was all for peace and, as we saw, soon afterwards played the last card by guaranteeing in his turn the Pragmatic Sanction. But George II's sentiments accorded entirely with Townshend's; and the armaments for which supplies were granted in 1729 and the subsidies were paid to Hesse-Cassel and Brunswick, were palpably not intended by the King for the defence of Gibraltar and Minorca, but for

action nearer home.   In other words, the political motive of
George II's journey to Hanover early in 1729 was to direct
the muster of troops on his electoral frontier, and in July
Prussia, who perfectly understood the meaning of the
demonstration, in return mobilised part of her army.

The difference was indeed settled without a resort to war,
King Frederick William I coming to terms notwithstanding
the pressure put upon him from both within and without,
and from Vienna itself, to make him persevere in his attitude
of defiance [1].   The genuinely pacific intentions of this conscientious prince, to which his son pays a very left-handed
acknowledgment [2], had not yet come to be thoroughly
appreciated ; and the result, which King George II attributed
solely to his own superior determination, sensibly added to
the self-consciousness which long exercised so potent an
influence upon the progress of our foreign policy.

After the resignation of Townshend in May 1730, however, Walpole's ascendancy in the guidance of foreign as
well as domestic affairs remained for a time undisputed.   In
the former department, no more signal success was achieved
by him than that of keeping Great Britain out of the War of
the Polish Succession, which broke out in 1733 and lasted
till 1735 (though the definitive treaty of peace was delayed
for three years further).   The credit due to Walpole for
having preserved Great Britain from participation in a conflict
that reduced *ad absurdum* the principle of an intervention
for the sake of safeguarding ulterior interests, is enhanced
by the fact that he found extreme difficulty in keeping the
King out of this war, both in 1734 and in the following year.
Lord Hervey [3] has given an elaborate account of the argu-

---

[1] As to the compromise see Stenzel, *Geschichte von Preussen*, vol. iii.
p. 568.

[2] *Histoire de mon temps*, ch. 11.

[3] *Memoirs*, vol. ii. pp. 38 seqq.

ments employed in a paper specially drawn up in 1734 by
' one Hatolf,' as he superciliously calls the Hanoverian
minister in London, in order to impress the Queen and
through her the King with the expediency of opposing France,
and takes note of the inclination towards this view shown by
both Secretaries of State, by the Duke of Grafton and others
—indeed, it would seem as if the majority of Walpole's own
Cabinet had been in agreement with royalty against him.
In 1735 this pressure was even more difficult to with-
stand, when, in spite of all efforts to the contrary on the
part of the entire ministry, the King had insisted on again
proceeding to Hanover.   It cannot be denied that the
anxiety of George II to strike a blow for the Emperor in
this quarrel was intelligible enough from the outset, since
its origin was a treaty of alliance, unprovoked by Austria,
but directed against her, between Spain and France, to
which, seizing upon the advantages of the situation with
frank promptitude, Charles Emmanuel III of Sardinia had
given in his adhesion.   As the war progressed, the ill
fortune of the Emperor's arms seemed to appeal still more
forcibly to the loyalty of the Elector, and the French seizure
of Kehl, which was a fortress of the Empire, formed a fresh
challenge to the members of that body.   Fortunately, the
reverses of the Emperor, and his intentness upon the
ultimate recognition of the Pragmatic Sanction by all the
European Powers, made him desirous of peace already in
the second year of the war ; or Walpole's rather cynical
summary of the results of the first year's campaign might not
have continued to satisfy the King and Queen : ' Madam, there
are fifty thousand men slain this year in Europe, and not
one Englishman [1].'   The scheme of pacification proposed
in the first instance by the British Government was, however,

---

[1] *Memoirs*, vol. ii. p. 62.

not accepted; and on its failure fresh pressure was put on King George by the Emperor to go into the war in accordance with his treaty obligations, and he was actually offered the command of the Imperial forces on the Rhine— an invitation well calculated as an appeal to his personal estimate of his powers although it neglected his incidental position as a British Sovereign[1]. Before the year was out, however, the bases of peace had been virtually settled, and after protracted negotiations they were brought to a formal conclusion in the Third Treaty of Vienna, in November, 1738. The evidence on which the credit of this settlement was given to Walpole is not altogether satisfactory; for although during part of this period (1736) Horace Walpole the elder, by a quite exceptional arrangement, attended the King as minister at Hanover in the place of Harrington, he is stated to have been 'as much for war as his brother was against it[2].' King George certainly took much pride in the pacification, although in more respects than one it ran counter to his former wishes. To be sure, in the matter of the succession to the Polish throne, which the war had nominally been waged to settle, he was gratified by the withdrawal of the *protégé* of France, Stanislas Lescynski, of whom he had disapproved. Austria further gained, besides what proved a precarious tenure of Parma and Piacenza, the French guarantee of the Pragmatic Sanction, and in return for these dynastic advantages conceded to France the reversion of Lorraine which the destined husband of the Pragmatic heiress exchanged for Tuscany. The eventual diminution of the strength of the Empire by the sacrifice of an important borderland was a consequence to which Walpole would of course have remained supremely in-

[1] *Memoirs*, vol. ii. pp. 178-9.
[2] *Ib.*, p. 43. Horace had laboured to bring over the authorities at the Hague to his opinion.

different. But until it has been ascertained from the Hanover archives whether Hattorf or any of his colleagues were alive to the ulterior importance of this arrangement, we must leave it undecided whether George II, warmly as he entered into the interests of the Empire, was justified of Adolf Schmidt and Treitschke, as I feel sure he was not of those readers of history who are revolted by the indifference to popular sentiments and interests shown in the territorial juggle of this notorious treaty.

In the Spanish War declared in November, 1739, into which Walpole was forced, partly by the unscrupulous tactics of the Opposition and partly by the rush of popular opinion which they had provoked, the Hanoverian Electorate had no conceivable cause of interest. The position of Great Britain was full of hazard; for she had no allies, even the United Provinces having been prevailed upon by France to hold aloof in a timid neutrality, while the Emperor Charles VI, sick to death and lost to any political thought but his long-cherished design of securely transmitting his possessions in their entirety to his elder daughter, remained indifferent to any other temptation[1]. Frederick William I of Prussia, in reply to British solicitations, roundly refused to be employed as a hack, and was in truth presciently desirous above all things of not alienating the good will of France. In a word, the British Government knocked at every door, but met with no response except at Copenhagen, whose Court was still bound to us by a subsidy-treaty, concluded in 1735 by way of demonstrating that we were prepared for any emergency. As to France herself, all doubts had vanished as to the existence of a close understanding between her and Spain, and she was known to be only

[1] Great Britain had suggested to him a possible recovery of Naples and Sicily, the provisions of the Third Treaty of Vienna being to this extent undone.

awaiting the most favourable opportunity for joining that Power in the war which we had declared against her.

Yet the country was all for war, and in none of his least responsible advisers was the combative impulse stronger than in the King himself. The approval bestowed by him upon the war must be mainly ascribed to his bellicose disposition, stimulated by the eloquent appeals addressed by Carteret and others to the same instinct in the nation at large. But the case was altered when, with the death of the Emperor Charles VI in October, 1770, six months after that of Frederick William I of Prussia in May, the crisis actually presented itself in which, as an Elector of the Empire, George II was directly interested, and when a conflict ensued that brought into question the security of his Electorate.

We have seen how time had left unmitigated the asperity of the personal relations between George II and his Prussian brother-in-law, although in some other respects the confidence of the latter in his convictions had been broken, and how it had become the consistent endeavour of both the French and the Austrian Government to keep the two Kings politically at variance [1]. In the later years of Frederick William, the East Frisian question kept up a continual irritation with the Hanoverian 'Government, and it is repeatedly referred to in the diplomatic correspondence of the period. But so far as I can see it would be wrong to ascribe the continuance of the royal ill-will against Prussia to Hanoverian influence exercised upon the King; with the exception of Walpole no English political leader advocated a reconciliation between him and Frederick William [2]; and as to the East Frisian dispute, the King's Hanoverian

[1] Horace Walpole to R. Trevor, June 20, 1738. (*Earl of Buckinghamshire's Papers*, in Historical MSS. Commission, Fourteenth Report, Appendix, Part IX.)

[2] Coxe, *Life of Lord Walpole*, vol. i. p. 425.

councillors were at one with his British ministers in recognising the expediency of a compromise : thus it was the
obstinate determination of the King to keep up the quarrel,
which prevailed over both sets of advisers [1].   But the intense
personality of the feeling on the part of George II, while, in
the language of a contemporary observer, it made him
'extremely averse to do anything that squints in the least
towards praising' the old King of Prussia, left the question
open as to whether the relation to his successor would be
a wholly different one.   Indeed, it had been suggested as
advisable to gain the good will of the heir to the Prussian
throne during his father's lifetime; and there are certain
indications, although I do not think they can be said to be
worth anything as evidence, that money intended as an
instalment of a pension to the Crown Prince was actually
sent to Berlin [2].   In any case Horace Walpole, whom we
must not take altogether at his nephew and namesake's
valuation, saw the situation clearly, when only a few days
before the death of Frederick William, he wrote that in his
opinion the future security of Europe would depend upon the
crisis now at hand, and upon England's gaining or not gaining
the new King of Prussia.   On the accession of Frederick II
the prospect, however, continued clouded.   The mediatory services of the Prussian Queen Dowager between her brother and
her son were both claimed and given, but remained ineffectual,
partly in consequence of the new King's excess of curiosity as
to family concerns hitherto hidden in a safe obscurity.   Nor,
as English statesmen felt, was a family reconciliation with
regard to the past so much at issue as a distinct political understanding with regard to the future.   France, whose struggle
with Great Britain for colonial empire was already at hand,

[1] Horace Walpole's *Letters to Trevor, u. s.,* May 23, 1740.
[2] *Ib., Introduction,* p. xv.

L

would find an almost insuperable obstacle to the aggressive policy which she was resuming in Europe, if an understanding between Great Britain and Prussia could be used at the last moment to bring the latter Power and Austria into agreement[1]. But all such hopes proved vain. When—only three months after the death of the Emperor Charles VI— in January, 1741, Frederick II unmasked his designs and openly stated the price at which he was willing to accept a settlement, his audacity in thus treating the Prussian guarantee of the Pragmatic Sanction astounded even those British politicians who were most sceptical as to the expediency of giving an uncompromising support to the Austrian claims. Yet before the outbreak of the War of the Succession, as well as afterwards, Walpole—or in justice to Horace I should say Walpole and his brother—continued to look for the best prospect of a general settlement in an accommodation between Austria and Prussia. But the great peace minister's day had nearly passed; and in the midst of the general collapse of his authority we hardly notice the failure of his attempt to prevent the King's journey to Hanover in 1741. Now that, under the influence of one of those waves of feeling which it is idle to talk of a minister's resisting, both King and nation were intent upon supporting the young Queen of Hungary in the trouble against which her father's guarantees had proved a futile fence, Walpole clung to the conviction that even her interests as well as those of the restoration of peace would be best served by a direct accommodation between her and the Prussian King. He had found himself obliged to move in Parliament the maintenance of our Pragmatic guarantee by means of an armed force and a subsidy of which the alliance of Hanover in July definitely fixed the amounts; but this was

[1] See Horace Walpole's *Letters to Trevor, u. s.,* pp. 31-2.

not incompatible with the endeavours in which he doubtless more willingly engaged, to detach Prussia from the rest of the adversaries of the Queen, and more especially of course from France. Was it incompatible with another transaction whereby, for the first time in the history of the Personal Union, the interests of the Hanoverian Electorate were openly and in the most marked fashion treated as separate from those of Great Britain? Before his Parliament King George II had adopted a warlike air, beyond a doubt in perfect harmony with his personal sentiments, referring to the Danish and Hesse-Cassel troops which by virtue of the subsidy treaties would enable him to carry out the stipulations of the Hanover Alliance[1]. But after he had—as already noticed—early in 1741, against the strong representations of Walpole, betaken himself to Hanover, in order to direct the military operations of his contingents and thus, we shall not err in concluding, utilise forces in British pay for at least partly electoral purposes, he found himself checkmated by the Franco-Prussian Alliance (June 4). In accordance with this agreement, one of the two French armies which crossed the Rhine in August threatened the Electorate from the West, and a Prussian division collected on the Elbe (near Magdeburg) to the South. The Elector was thus placed in direct danger, and on September 27 he concluded the treaty of neutrality, by which he bound himself to abstain from assisting the Queen of Hungary, and pledged himself in the approaching Imperial election not to vote for her husband Duke Francis Stephen of Lorraine.

Few transactions, if any, for which the Hanoverian *régime* was responsible—for Kloster Zeven, as we shall see, was only a military convention, and was moreover rejected by the

---

[1] The Danish treaty had however only a year to run, after which the Danes were bound by a similar treaty to France.

Sovereign—raised a storm of obloquy comparable to that of the neutrality treaty of 1741.

The satirical wit of the age—no very nice variety of this class of effort—exploded its preparations, in the form of vapid parody and doggrel ballad [1]; Lord Marchmont produced a pamphlet; Lord Chesterfield bent himself double in epigram; and Newcastle proposed in the Cabinet a remonstrance which has the uncompromising sound of an amendment proposed by an irresponsible fraction in the House of Commons to the address on the speech from the Throne [2]. It is not, one must confess, easy to defend the Treaty of Neutrality; yet it seems tolerably clear that, had Walpole in the wane of his power ventured to breast the tide, a treaty of British instead of Hanoverian neutrality (such as the French Government actually pressed for) would have well suited the plan upon which his Government was actually intent. British diplomacy obtained from Frederick II the secret compromise of Kleinschnellendorf (October, 1741); and after he had ignored this agreement, it was again the British Government which guaranteed the preliminaries of Breslau (June, 1742), and thus materially helped to bring about the Peace of Berlin, that ended the First Silesian War (July).

[1] Sir Charles Hanbury Williams's *Old England's Te Deum* is preserved in his *Works*; see Lord Orford's *Letters*, vol. i. p. 85.

[2] For the circumstances of the conclusion of this treaty and the reception given to it by the Cabinet, see G. Harris's *Life of Lord Hardwicke* (1847), vol. i. p. 519. The secrecy with which the King had concluded it was in the eyes of the British Government as objectionable as the treaty itself. Newcastle, besides proposing a remonstrance to be sent to Harrington with a request that the King would reconsider his action, proposed to inform the European Courts that, as King of Great Britain, His Majesty would adhere to his engagements with Austria, and use his best endeavours in her support. This proposal, however, which would have thrown a strange light upon the perversities of the Personal Union, commended itself neither to Walpole nor to his colleagues; and the incident terminated with a threat of resignation by Newcastle, which cannot have been generally expected to be carried out.

But before this Walpole's fall had taken place, and the current of public feeling in favour of Maria Theresa had begun to set in, which in the following year (1743) resulted in the armed intervention of Great Britain on behalf of the Pragmatic Cause, and the appearance in the field of the King-Elector in person. Thus, the Treaty of Neutrality had been concluded doubly in vain, and had in the end served no permanent purpose of either British or Hanoverian policy.

Walpole's fall (February, 1742) brought into power as Secretary of State (for the Northern Department) a politician whom it is a mistake to represent as blindly devoted to the interests of the House of Habsburg, but whose sympathies were strong with the old Whig system of resistance to France in alliance with Austria. Carteret had already in the previous reign, when he was joint Secretary with Townshend, roused the spleen of his ' brother ' (to use Townshend's term of official affection[1]) by seeking the support at Hanover of Bernstorff, whose influence was then declining, and of certain ladies of the Court. He had furthermore, with the aid of his exceptional proficiency in the German tongue, acquired that knowledge of the German dynasties which King George II regarded as the beginning of wisdom. Thus, although he had when in opposition felt constrained to support the interests of the Prince of Wales, even this was forgiven by the King to a politician so much after his own heart; and it was probably Walpole's knowledge of the desire cherished at Court to bring Carteret back into office which caused his jealous distrust of this opponent to excite in him a degree of animosity such as neither the vehemence of Pulteney nor the malice of Chesterfield was capable of provoking. Not long

[1] See Townshend's letter to Sir Robert Walpole, *s. d.*, printed from the *Hardwicke Papers* in the Appendix to Coxe's *Life of Walpole*, vol. ii. pp. 402-6.

before her death in 1737 Queen Caroline informed Walpole
of Carteret's having protested that he had only taken up
his stand against the Prime Minister because refused admit-
tance by him into his ministry; to which Sir Robert,
with more than his usual bluntness, rejoined that 'it was
impossible the King's business could go on long with him
and Lord Carteret both in the King's service,' and offered to
quit himself so as to make things easy [1].   And later in the
same year, after Carteret's display of fidelity towards the
interests of the Prince of Wales, Walpole repeated his resolve
never in any way to 'act with that man [2].'   Partly, no doubt,
he feared that Carteret, if admitted into his Government,
would entirely undermine his influence at Court; but he
must also have felt himself at variance with this possible
rival as to the guiding motives of the national foreign policy.
Frequently as Walpole had shifted his position, more especially since his parting with Townshend had left the control
of foreign affairs more completely in his own hands, he had
always regarded the alliance with France as the corner-stone
of the system to be maintained.   Nor is he to be censured
because the progress of enterprise beyond the seas, to which
the commercial spirit fostered by his own policy of peace
had materially contributed, was rendering a collision with
France as inevitable as the quarrel with Spain had proved,
and this at the very time when Fleury's control over French
policy was loosening.   To Walpole's profound distrust of
the House of Austria, on which historians have perhaps
insufficiently dwelt, I have more than once directed your
attention.   Carteret, on the other hand, in the great speech
with which on the occasion of the celebrated two-edged
motion for the dismissal of Walpole he led the assault in the
Lords, insisted above all on the vacillation and impotence

---

[1] Lord Hervey's *Memoirs*, vol. iii. p. 95.   [2] *Ib.*, p. 297.

of the minister in the face of the persistent aggressiveness
of France and of her encroachments upon the integrity of
the Empire[1]. The Treaty of Nymphenburg (May, 1741)
seemed to justify this view so fully as to cause Walpole to
bow before it; and though before his fall German affairs took
a pacific turn, the current to which he had yielded was still
as strong as ever when Carteret, whose own sympathies all
flowed in the same direction, found himself at last again in
office.

Although Carteret had never sat in the House of Commons, he had in a sphere not then so tranquil as it has since
become found room for the constant exercise of his oratorical
powers, which are easily recognisable in his voluminous written
remains He never seems at a loss for ideas, and was always
capable of developing them with both amplitude and lucidity.
His clearness of insight is unmistakeable; and in Ireland he
had given signal proof of what Swift calls a genteel manner,
or as we might put it, of that grand air which exercises an
irresistible fascination over so many ordinary mortals. I have
already spoken of his linguistic accomplishments, which were
wider in range than those of the gentlemanly scholarship of
his day, though in this too he excelled. But notwithstanding
his high personal and political reputation, his rare accomplishments to which I have already adverted, and an unconcealed self-esteem which was transparent to Queen Caroline
but probably did him no harm with the public, Carteret
never commended himself to Parliament or popular opinion
as a possible head of the Government, although at a much
later date (in 1756) the Duke of Newcastle tried to put him
in that position and thus keep himself in office. The truth
is that Carteret's openly expressed contempt for popular
institutions was repaid by a more or less vague distrust

---

[1] Ballantyne, *u. s.*, p. 225.

which it would be unjust to ascribe wholly to his supposed openness to Hanoverian influences, of which too much has probably been made. He was quite out of touch with a House of Commons which he never made it part of his business to bring under control by those influences of which Newcastle was master; and as it happened he never had a seat there himself. But it may be well to note that even his conduct of foreign affairs—for with Newcastle as his colleague this was in his hands so long as Lord Wilmington was at the head of the Government, and afterwards until his final rupture with Pelham—lacked the support which has been commanded by every really great foreign minister. As in an autocracy the prince, so in a free polity Parliament and people must repose in the conductor of their foreign policy that personal trust which implies convinced deference, if his voice and action are to become heard and felt as theirs. Moreover Carteret's tenure of power, such as it was, was short; it is to be counted by months, not by years, of which it lasted not quite two, and the attempt to revive it in 1746, when Lords Granville and Bath held the seals of the two Secretaryships for forty-eight hours and some odd minutes, would have covered him with ridicule, if he had shown the least concern in the *fiasco*. Yet Carteret's administration of foreign affairs possesses special interest for us in connexion with our immediate subject, as covering a brief period during which the dynastic policy of the House of Hanover, incarnate in King George II, was at one with the impulses which were both consciously animating the nation, and half unconsciously urging it onward to the establishment of its world-empire; so that I shall ask permission to make some brief reference to it at the beginning of my next lecture.

LECTURE V

WHEN, early in 1742, Carteret at last found himself
in possession of the seals, he had succeeded to the
heritage of a policy which had settled down into the support
of the Pragmatic Heiress by the British Government, while
it had reluctantly assented to the withdrawal of the Electorate
from immediate peril. In the last months of the war, when
even Russia had, by the sudden advent to the throne of the
Czarina Elisabeth, come under the rule of a friend of France,
the Queen of Hungary had no extraneous support but the
gold which Great Britain poured into her treasury. Something more than the payment of subsidies had however been
looked for from Carteret in many quarters, and had probably
been intended by himself. He told Wasner, the able
Austrian Resident in London, who was at that time very
actively endeavouring to promote a declaration of war by
Great Britain against France, that he was certainly not
Prussian in his sentiments, but a good Englishman, which
was as much as saying, a good Austrian. And certainly
this description of himself is borne out by the instructions
with which he supplied Lord Hyndford when, a few weeks
after taking office, and following in the first instance
Walpole's policy of attempting to bring about a reconciliation between Austria and Prussia, he charged that long-
suffering diplomatist with a pacific mission to Breslau, while
Sir Thomas Robinson was directed to make fresh efforts at

Vienna. Carteret's state papers at times have about them
that air of extreme frankness in which only very great
statesmen can indulge without laying themselves open to
sarcastic comment; nor is it easy to understand why Lord
Hyndford, whose personal views seem to have on the whole
coincided with Carteret's, should not have been trusted to
read more largely between the lines. ' The King is prepared
to stand by and support the House of Austria, and is
equipping a body of 16,000 men. . . . The King of Prussia
is mistaken, if instead of making terms with Austria he goes
to war [in alliance] with France; he will only be known
as a Destroyer of Germany, and France will not (if they are
successful) suffer him, a Protestant prince and a natural
enemy, to share the spoils. In the opposite event (if he
makes a reasonable peace with Austria), he will be sure of
the support of the Maritime Powers. We can never suffer
the Emperor to remain master of Bohemia or see it in any
other hands than the Austrian family.' And then, after
an edifying reference to the sagacious self-interestedness of
Sardinia, ' The King would gladly see the King of Prussia
engaged in the actual support of the House of Austria ' ; but
it must be in the way which suits us best ; ' as for taking his
troops into our pay, we cannot do it ; and unless he has totally
deserted the former principles of his family,' he will assuredly
not make such a demand. In a general way, ' negotiating
with him we hold to be extremely dangerous ; and your
Lordship must have the greatest guard upon yourself in
conferring with him. . . . We will support him if he will
agree with the Queen of Hungary; but we cannot enter
into any notions of procuring advantages for our allies.'
And the hectoring spirit of these instructions reaches its
climax in the arrogant refusal which follows to go even so
far as to consult beforehand the Power whose co-operation
will be tolerated : ' nor does the King want to be taught

by them (his allies) in what way the schemes of France
may be best disappointed[1].'

Yet although it might seem as if negotiations begun in
such a spirit could not have had much prospect of success,
they were probably not quite hopeless even before the
course of events rendered Lord Hyndford's arguments
irresistible. Maria Theresa seems to have been disposed
to cede the whole of Silesia to Frederick if only she could
obtain from him satisfactory assurances as to his bearing
after the cession. But the distrust of Frederick had gone
too deep; and at Vienna regret was openly expressed to
Robinson that in England any credit should be allowed to
the King of Prussia for honesty of intentions. But in the
midst of the negotiations the battle of Chotusitz (Czaslau)
was fought (May 17, 1742), of which Arneth aptly says that
it was 'with perfect justice called a Prussian victory, though
it would be going too far to call it an Austrian defeat,' and
which would thus seem to have raised the respect of each side
for the other. The Preliminaries of Breslau were accordingly
concluded, and succeeded by the conclusion of peace at
Berlin, which left the French under Belle-Isle to extricate
themselves as best they could from Bohemia. Of this peace
Frederick the Great calls Carteret the interested promoter[2];
but if, as I am certainly disposed to think, it may be regarded
as the most successful achievement of his administration of
foreign affairs, this commendation by no means extends to
the attitude subsequently maintained by the British Government. The treaty of peace had indeed brought about
a settlement between Austria and Prussia; but although the
honour of the former had been preserved, she had lost one
of the fairest of her provinces. Upon France a bitter

[1] *Instructions to Lord Hyndford in setting forth to the King of
Prussia*, March 30, 1742, in *British Museum Additional MSS.*, 22,531.
[2] *Histoire de mon temps*, ch. vii.

humiliation had been inflicted, which to Cardinal Fleury
was only assuaged by the satisfaction which springs from
a fulfilled prediction of misfortune. She was unlikely to
forgive the Power which had so actively promoted, and had
together with the United Provinces and Russia guaranteed,
the Treaty of Berlin.

But after Carteret had so judiciously counselled Maria
Theresa against her own impulses, and had successfully
crossed the designs of France, he should have endeavoured
in the sequel to prevent the latter Power from finding an
opportunity of regaining the vantage-ground of which she had
thus been deprived. Maria Theresa, while not prepared to
break the compact to which she had assented, was known to
be weeping bitter tears for a loss which might still admit of
being made good should the violation of engagements proceed from the other side. In a word, every effort ought to
have been made by the British Government to avert a renewal of the alliance between France and Prussia. But the
surest way to bring about such a renewal was by strengthening the resources, and increasing the confidence of Austria
to such an extent as to excite the apprehensions both of
her present and of her recent adversary. Such, however,
was precisely the effect of Carteret's action. What was it
to Great Britain that the House of Austria should aspire not
only to hold its own, but to rise once more to its undisputed supremacy in Germany, and that while the wound
inflicted by the seizure of Silesia remained unhealed, schemes
should be laid at Vienna for recovering Alsace and Lorraine
for the Empire with the aid of our subsidies and soldiers?
If this was an object legitimately of value ʾɔ an Elector of
the Empire, the pursuit of it was at the same time certain
to imperil the security of the Electorate, and to involve a
continuous and heavy expenditure. The whole policy was
one to whose purpose it was not easy to find an end, and

of whose cost it might prove arduous to reach the bottom.
Indeed, Carteret's way of thinking (which reflects itself in
his way of writing) inclines one to suspect that this very
grandeur of range commended it to him, just as it was likewise in harmony with the imperialist ideas of Münchhausen,
a statesman already at this date much in the confidence of
the King, and with George II's own military ambition.

When in 1743, everything going well with Austria, the
army which had in the previous year been massed in Flanders
was at the request of our ally marched into the Empire, the
question was naturally enough asked: for whose sake was
this large and in part illegally engaged force taking the field?[1]
In answer to the clamour which arose that the extraordinary
effort made by Great Britain was being utilised solely for
Hanoverian interests, Lord Chancellor Hardwicke, certainly
the ablest dialectician in the Cabinet, contended that so far
from Great Britain being sacrificed to Hanover, Hanover
was evidently 'hazarded by her union with Great Britain.'
The truth of the general proposition was undeniable, that by
the circumstances of the Personal Union Hanover was more
likely to be imperilled by the action of her predominant
partner than vice versa ; indeed, the observation, which in a
general way runs glibly off the pens of Hanoverian historians,
applies very forcibly to the later period of the connexion,
on which I fear it will be impossible to touch except in

---

[1] The army numbered 70,000 men, who included, together with the
6,000 Hessians in British pay under Walpole's subsidy-treaty, 16,000
Hanoverians. There can be no doubt as to the unlawfulness of their
engagement without the consent of Parliament, which was not sitting at
the time. The plea of necessity could hardly have been raised at a time
when the King of Prussia was declaring that if the British army crossed
from Flanders into the Empire he would in turn march upon the Hanoverian frontier. The defensive treaty (usually called the First Treaty of
Hanover) concluded in November with Prussia was merely a device for
keeping her quiet until her protests might be safely ignored.

the briefest possible way within the compass of these lectures.
The Napoleonic age apart, even in the Seven Years' War,
when 'America was conquered in Germany,' Hanover (and
Brunswick with her) had to bear a wholly disproportionate
share of the sufferings entailed by a struggle waged by Great
Britain for the interests of her empire at large. But in the
Pragmatic War as such it could not and cannot be contended
with candour that Great Britain, though placed under obligations by her guarantee, had any real interests of her own at
stake. Carteret knew this when he boldly justified it as a war
with France, though when her declaration followed he could
find no words strong enough to describe her insolence and
mendacity[1]. The proposal of Prussia that the Empire should
be left to defend its own inviolability he loftily waved aside,
and at the end of February, 1743, the British march began.

When four months later the Tower guns saluted the
great victory of Dettingen, and Handel's strains thanked
the God of battles for His grace, some critical spirits hinted
that since we had been auxiliaries only, we ought not to be
as pleased and as proud as if we had been principals. Had
the victory, however, been followed up by the invasion of
France which was actually planned, the war would have at
once revealed itself in a new character and have justified
itself to the nation as an integral part of the struggle for
empire with France. As it was, the French soon evacuated
Germany, and the British camp became the scene of futile
negotiations for settling the affairs of the Empire. Perhaps
the most striking episode, but at the same time the least
satisfactorily explained in the records of Carteret's direct
activity after Dettingen, is the attempt to solve the German
question by a compromise with the unfortunate Emperor
Charles VII. This effort was certainly countenanced by

[1] See his letter to Robinson, March, 1744, *British Museum Additional MSS.*, 22,529, p. 305.

Carteret in the first instance ; but apparently he afterwards
dropped the project without having secured for it a fair
attention either in Vienna or, which would have been more
immediately to the purpose, in London.   The long but very
clear statement of Prince William of Hesse-Cassel, preserved
among the Carteret papers in the British Museum[1], cannot
I fear be analysed in a few words.   Its purpose, however, was
to secure to the Emperor a retreat from a hopeless position on
the twofold basis of the retention of his Bavarian dominions
and—though this was of course not expressed—a retention of
the Imperial dignity.   Obviously, he could not continue to
hold the latter unless at least the greater part of his Electorate
was restored to him ; and the difficulties of such a concession
were in fact slighter than those which must have attended
any alternative arrangement of the kind said to have occurred
to Carteret, of establishing him in Naples or in some
dominion to be taken from France.   The assent in principle
which Carteret seems at first to have given to the proposal
was accordingly not the less statesmanlike because it was
generous.   But, contrary to his usual *coûte que coûte* habit
of political thought, he appears to have abandoned the
scheme with the same facility with which he had in the first
instance welcomed it, perhaps after satisfying himself at first-
hand that it was impossible to look for its acceptance at
Vienna.   Whether or not he withheld a knowledge of
this transaction from the ministry at home, where a change
adverse to him was in preparation and his colleague the
Duke of Newcastle was against all compromise as to the
Imperial title[2], it remained a *coup manqué*.   Yet though in
July, 1743, Henry Pelham became Prime Minister, and

---

[1] *British Museum Additional MSS.*, 22,527, pp. 289 seqq.   The
Prince acted as Regent for his brother the King of Sweden, whom he
afterwards succeeded as Landgrave William VIII.

[2] Coxe's *Life of Pelham*, vol. i. p. 87.

Carteret, who had supported the pretensions of Bath (Pulteney), must have become conscious of the insecurity of his own tenure of power, he now fell back, in accordance with the sentiments of the royal victor of Dettingen, upon an uncompromising support of Austria. The Treaty of Worms (September), which added Sardinia to the list of Powers subsidised by Great Britain, and indefinitely prolonged the Austrian subsidy[1], not only resembled the beginning of a new Grand Alliance, but it included a guarantee of all the territories which the House of Austria possessed or to which it was entitled, thus nullifying the guarantee of the possession of Silesia accorded to Prussia in the Treaty of Berlin. George II and Carteret, whose agreement was now complete, stretched their demands upon the submissiveness of ministry and Parliament to the uttermost limit; it is a kinsman of Lord Hardwicke, no peevish or inflexible officer of state, who reports that when he as Lord Chancellor refused in Council to attach the Great Seal to the Treaty of Worms, Carteret exclaimed that the King should affix it himself[2]. The letter which Frederick the Great afterwards charged George II with having written *manu propriâ*, in order to encourage Maria Theresa to take thought of the actual recovery of Silesia, was said to have been sent at a rather earlier date

---

[1] This promise, contained in a supplementary conviction however, was virtually repudiated by the Government at home.

[2] The letter, mentioned in the *Histoire de mon temps*, is in a royal rescript to Podewils, dated 'immediately after the signing of the Peace of Breslau' (Droysen, vol. v. part ii. p. 224, *note*). There seems no reason for supposing British influence to have had any concern in the endeavour to force the Diet of the Empire to second Austria's protest against the election and rule of the Emperor Charles VII (the so-called *Dictaturstreit*) ; it had however the support of Hanover, and I should suspect in this the hand of Münchhausen. The ominous conclusion of a treaty of alliance between Austria and Saxony, formerly one of the anti-Pragmatic Allies (December, 1743), was expressly attributed to British efforts (*ib.*, p. 203).

in Carteret's period of office ; but there are other indications
that towards the close of that period Great Britain, as the associate of a Power bent upon *revanche*, was steadily pursuing
a course which could not but necessitate great national efforts
and sacrifices.   Yet the Austrian cause had ceased to be
popular with either Parliament or people, and the determination of the Crown to support it could only endure, so long as
a ministry could be found to continue the requisite measures.
But at the head of the Government now stood Henry Pelham,
a politician who was himself the embodiment of caution,
and whose finger was always on the pulse of Parliament.

For a time the unpopularity of the policy of which Carteret
continued to be the agent, and of which he was the only resolute upholder, chiefly took the concrete form of opposition to
the employment of Hanoverian troops in the British service ;
but it soon deepened into a bitter resentment of the entire
' Hanoverian ' influence traceable in the policy of the country,
or, in other words, of the part played by the King in the conduct of public affairs. The unpopularity of the dynasty seemed
by the spring of 1744 to have become so established a fact
that the war party in France, which had now possessed itself
of the control of affairs there, thought its opportunity come
at last.   War was declared by France in March, and during
the next few weeks England was threatened with a French
invasion.   The menace was met with high spirit, and the
apprehension soon passed.   But the policy of the King and
Carteret was to bear further fruit.   In May the conclusion
of the Union of Frankfort announced that Frederick II of
Prussia had once more joined the supporters of the Emperor
Charles VII, and in June his alliance with France was concluded.   In the same month he took possession of East Frisia,
so long the object of Hanoverian desires, on the death of
its last native prince.   In August he gave a still more striking
proof of that promptitude which was the most characteristic

M

of all his qualities in action, by marching into Bohemia and thus opening the second Silesian War.

The earlier events of that war proved unexpectedly favourable to the cause of Maria Theresa, and the sudden death of the Emperor Charles VII in January, 1745, was an advantage which of course could not have been calculated upon. But before this event happened, the ill-will which had accumulated against King George and Carteret had at last been visited upon the minister's head. His openness of purpose and frankness of speech had become arrogant self-assertion; 'with the Crown on his side,' he avowed his belief that he could defy the keen wit of Chesterfield, the rushing eloquence of Pitt, and the hesitations of his own colleagues the Pelhams, and force them to leave him—what he openly demanded—a free hand[1]. When in former days, during his embassy in Sweden, the settlement agreed upon between himself and the Queen and her consort had been delayed by the estates, for whom the so-called 'period of liberty' was in those troubled days opening, he had with his habitual vehemence exclaimed against the difficulties inseparable from 'popular' methods of government. The chief of these 'difficulties' was to form the rock upon which his attempt to remain the King's foreign minister in the teeth of Parliament went to pieces. His conduct of affairs had in an unusual degree depended on the money-granting factor in the State; yet in the House of Commons he was without power or influence. The payment of the Hanoverians in the British service, and the network of subsidy-treaties, of which the most recent with Saxony had been concluded mainly with the view of bringing over a formerly hostile Power to the Austrian side, were themes which the Commons had a primary right to discuss, and to which they returned with unflagging interest. Thus the question

---

[1] *Stanhope*, vol. iii. p. 185, *note*, from Horace Walpole.

whether Carteret—now Earl Granville—should stay in office
or go, became in the last resort a constitutional one, involving
a decision between the personal preferences of the dynasty
and the claim of the nation to control the provision for its
armaments. As if to emphasise this view of the case,
Frederick Prince of Wales for once joined hands with his
father in the attempt to maintain Granville, and in urging
his removal Orford rendered a last service to the dynasty.
Thus, on the eve of the Rebellion that so unexpectedly
shook the throne, an English statesman of great ability and
high aspirations fell from power, who had done more than
any Hanoverian minister before or after him to make his
countrymen denounce the Personal Union. For it was owing
to this Union that Carteret's master seemed to have become
wholly unable to act or think as a British King.

Carteret's fall would point a more impressive moral, had it
been followed by any speedy change in our system of policy
or in the method of carrying out that upon which we had
entered. Nothing of the kind was to be expected either
from the Pelhams or from Harrington, who returned to office
in Lord Granville's place, and nothing of the kind was dreamt
of by the King. Our engagements remained, and even Pitt,
who gave a general support to the Government in which no
suitable office had been found for him, abstained from insisting
on more than that the war should not be carried on till the
aspirations of the House of Austria should have been
satisfied. Under these circumstances the subsidy system was,
after a nominal stoppage of the payment of the Hanoverian
and Hessian troops, continued and even extended by the
Pelham Government; and Saxony, together with two Spiritual
Electors, enjoyed British pay. The King's mood, moreover,
was more difficult than ever, now that none of his English
advisers had his full personal confidence, while the Hanoverian
influence upon him was at this time remarkably strong. In

1745 he paid a visit to Hanover, against the desire of all who wished him well in England ; while here his personal treatment of his ministers had been such that the Cabinet addressed to him a dutiful remonstrance on the subject, of which he took not the slightest notice [1].   Yet on the whole it may be said that the British ministry was beginning to relax the bonds of alliance with Austria without essaying as yet to shake them off, and that they thus acted in conscious disregard of the wishes of the King and his Hanoverian adviser Münch-hausen.   The successes of France and Prussia, and the experiences of the insurrection in the north, might have induced even Carteret, had he still been in office, to fall back upon his earlier and more prudent method of seeking to checkmate France by detaching Prussia from her alliance, rather than to keep Prussia true to it by exciting Austria against her.   At all events, the Pelham administration was by August, 1745, prepared to enter into the Secret Convention of Hanover (negotiated there by Harrington under the eye of George II himself), which exhibits Great Britain once more in the position of a mediatress, renewing the old stipulations of the treaties of Breslau and Berlin, with the reasonable addition of the promise of the Brandenburg vote in favour of Maria Theresa's consort at the imminent election to the Imperial throne.   The events of the year made a policy of moderation imperative :   the Duke of Cumberland had very gallantly suffered defeat at Fontenoy (May) ;   not long afterwards his troops were wanted in the Highlands ;   and both the United Provinces and Sardinia were yielding to the allurements of peace with profit.   Thus Maria Theresa was actually forced into the Peace of Dresden (December) by the refusal of the British Government to continue its subsidies if she declined to come to terms with her Prussian adversary.   The alliance

---

[1] *Life of Hardwicke*, vol. iii. pp. 125 and 143.

between Austria and Great Britain had therefore left unsatis-
fied Maria Theresa's aspirations for the recovery of her lost
province.   Three furthei years sufficed to show that it had
been equally unable to hasten the success of Great Britain in
her struggle with France, of which it had precipitated the
outbreak.   The reverses suffered by the allies in Flanders
after the return thither of the victor of Culloden, were held
of greater account than the British victories on the high seas,
and in the Peace of Aix-la-Chapelle (October, 1748), which
ended the so-called War of the Austrian Succession, Great
Britain consented to relinquish at least one acquisition which
the requirements of her Imperial expansion could ill spare,
and to adjourn the contest with France on whose final
results her future as a world-power depended.   But what
made this Peace obnoxious to George II and his Hanoverian
councillors was no insight on their part into its imperfections
on this head.   They disapproved of it because it implied
the failure of the policy which they had consistently upheld,
and which they could not bring themselves to lay aside.
Yet the day of that policy was near to its end.   The Peace
of Aix-la-Chapelle marks the breakdown, from the British as
well as from the Austrian point of view—and from the former
quite as conclusively as from the latter—of an alliance
dictated primarily by Hanoverian traditions and sympathies,
and vigorously upheld by Carteret alone among English
politicians of high mark, in obedience to impulses not dictated
by true statesmanship.   And it condemns him as severely as
if the humiliation had actually been imposed upon him of
being one of its signatories.

In what has gone before, the incidental mention of the
name of Münchhausen may have recalled to you how about
the time (or a little before it) when George II exchanged the
weakened control of Walpole for the acceptable services of
Carteret, he began to lean more and more habitually on the

counsels of this eminent Hanoverian statesman. The name
of Münchhausen in fact marks this chapter of the history
of Hanoverian influence upon British policy exercised
through the person of the Sovereign, as the names of
Bernstorff and Bothmer in a more direct way mark the
period covering the larger half of the reign of George I,
and as in yet another fashion Münster's connects itself dis-
tinctively with the later years of the reign of George III and
with the Regency. At the same time it is right to point out
that the documentary evidence on which alone the actual
extent of Münchhausen's influence in matters of foreign
policy could be established has not as yet found its way
into print; and probably nothing would be better worth
while than a systematic inspection of the ministerial and
London Chancery archives at Hanover with a view to
ascertaining what they contain on the subject. Baron
Gerlach Adolf von Münchhausen was clearly a statesman of
a very different intellectual type from that represented by
Bernstorff, while in the breadth and loftiness of their ideals
there were some resemblances between him and Münster.
Münchhausen is most widely remembered for an achievement of which the lasting credit is in a large measure due
to him, and to which it would not be possible in these
surroundings to refer without a word of cordial recognition.
For in truth it is not easy to recall an instance of the
foundation of a great modern University—unless it be that
of the University of Berlin, with which the fame of William
von Humboldt is similarly associated—in which the full
significance of the act has been so vividly present to the
mind of the virtual founder[1].

Münchhausen's opportunities of communication with his

---

[1] An admirable account of Münchhausen, by F. Frensdorff, is given
in vol. xxii of the *Allgemeine Deutsche Biographie,* and I have found
much illustrative matter concerning the earlier history of Göttingen in

Sovereign were doubtless very considerably increased when
in 1749 his younger brother Philip Adolf was appointed

a series of biographical papers entitled *Göttinger Professoren* (Gotha,
1872).

Münchhausen, whose family was of old Hanoverian origin (he belonged to the same line of it as a contemporary namesake whose adven-
tures were actually recommended to the British public on the ground of
his relationship to the celebrated minister), was born at Berlin, but entered
the Hanoverian service as early as 1715. It was not, however, till the
accession of George II that he became a member of the Privy Council—
the governing body, as we have seen, of the Electorate. His labours in this
capacity were during his earlier years of office mainly devoted to religious
and educational affairs, and thus he naturally came to occupy himself
with the idea of the foundation of a University which should be situate
within the new Electorate and proper to it. (The joint University of
Helmstädt, which necessarily declined in numbers on the foundation of
Göttingen, was abolished by King Jerome in 1810.)   The idea had
been originally thrown out, although in a rather different form, by
Leibniz, and such encouragement as it received in the uncongenial surroundings of the Court of George II was probably due to Queen
Caroline, the youngest of the princesses who prided themselves on their
intellectual indebtedness to the great thinker. It seems to have been
broached in Council by Münchhausen about 1731, to have been first officially taken up on the King's visit to Hanover in the following year, and to
have been carried out between 1734 and 1737, when the new University
was formally opened. Göttingen was very far from starting, like the
University of Berlin at a later day, equipped in her panoply; indeed
Frederick William I of Prussia had with vigilant jealousy threatened
with heavy penalties any professor who should allow himself to be
tempted away from Halle, and the Saxon princes, Albertine and
Ernestine, quickly followed suit on behalf of their Universities of
Leipzig, Wittenberg, and Jena. But the resoluteness of Münchhausen,
and the extraordinary insight displayed by him into the requirements of
the University from both the highest and the most practical points of
view, prevailed over all obstacles, and before the middle of the century
Göttingen had unmistakeably reached a stage of its progress when
promise was already ripening into fulfilment.   The solidity of its
administrative system thus combined with the reputation of its teachers,
among whom Mosheim, Haller, and Gesner belonged to this early period
of its history, to carry it safely through the troubles of the Seven Years'
War, after which began a long-continued era of prosperity on which

minister in attendance in London, and thus became head of
the German Chancery there.   The younger Münchhausen

I must abstain from dwelling.   But it may be to the purpose to remind
you that the academical history of Göttingen had from the first reflected
the ideas of its founder, and that, apart from other developements which
must here be passed by, it had consistently aimed at being a seminary
of statesmen and administrators ; for to the consciousness of this purpose must be in part attributed the conservative character which the
University maintained in the later Pre-Revolutionary days.   It had no
doubt been hoped that the connexion of Hanover with this country
would have the effect of inducing young Englishmen of position in
increasing numbers to pursue their studies at Göttingen ; but I cannot
perceive that such an effect ensued, at least for a considerable time to
come.   Yet Chesterfield, who took so very unflattering a view of the
benefits to be gained from a sojourn at either of our English Universities, was one of those who lent his countenance to the fashion, which
seems to have set in towards the close of George II's reign, of sending
young men of family to study international law at Leipzig under Mascov,
a former Göttingen professor no longer in his prime.   (Cf. Mason's
Memoirs of Whitehead, in Whitehead's *Works*, vol. iii. pp. 79–80.)
Göttingen only very gradually succeeded in attracting young Englishmen ; perhaps it did so to a greater extent after several of the sons of
George III had attended the University.   But I take it that such English
students as frequented the professors' lecture-rooms in the days when
Coleridge repaired to Göttingen to ' study the Kantian philosophy,' were
attracted less by the reputation of cameralists and constitutional historians such as Pütter, than by the fame of the eminent biologist and
physiologist Blumenbach, of the speculative theologian Eichhorn, and
perhaps of the great classical philologist Heyne.   The former two professors were attended by Coleridge ; there appear, however, to have been
but few of his countrymen studying at Göttingen with him, although
the practice of resorting to this place of learning seems not to have been
uncommon among young Englishmen, few of whom can have found it
as easy as he did to assimilate their habits of life and thought to German
ways.   (See Dr. Clement Carlyon's *Early Years and Late Reflections*,
1856, vol. i. pp. 16 seqq.)   On the other hand, all through the earlier
part of the reign of George III, Göttingen seems, curiously enough, to
have helped to anglicise the Hanoverian nobility and upper classes
whose sons so largely frequented the University ; the use of English had
gained much ground among the professors—in particular, as was natural
enough, from an early date among the leading members of the
flourishing medical faculty (see the letters from Werlhof to the cele-

seems to have held office till 1762; and it is not always
easy to distinguish between him and his brother, more especially as a thorough agreement in opinions and a perfect mutual
confidence is stated to have obtained between them[1].   The
elder brother remained for the most part at Hanover, although
he held important temporary positions such as that of Hanoverian Ambassador on the occasions of the elections of Charles
VII and Francis I to the Imperial throne in 1742 and 1745
respectively; nor was it till 1765 that he was formally placed
at the head of the Privy Council.   His influence upon the
Government of George II was consistently exerted in favour
as against Prussia, and of Austria for the maintenance of the
ancient position of the House of Austria in the Empire.   At
the same time, though opposed to the general policy of
Frederick II, and to the process of solution applied by him
to the constitutional system of the Empire, Münchhausen
appears to have been actuated by no such motives as were
uppermost in the mind of George II—an insatiable appetite
for territorial acquisitions, even of the pettiest sort, in
augmentation of his Hanoverian patrimony, and a violent
jealousy of Prussia.   These annexations were constantly
occupying the attention of George II, even at seasons of

brated Haller, printed by Frensdorff in *Zeitschrift des histor. Vereins
für Niedersachsen*, 1891, pp. 103 seqq.); and there can be no doubt
that the *genius loci* was highly favourable to influences primarily due to
the fact of the Personal Union.

Münchhausen died as an octogenarian in 1770, having enjoyed the
full confidence of George III, as well as that of his predecessor.

[1] The younger brother must be the Münchhausen referred to by Lord
Waldegrave (*Memoirs*, p. 29) when describing Cresset, secretary to
the Princess of Wales and her principal adviser up to about 1755, as
'uncommonly skilful in the politics of the backstairs, trusted by Lady
Yarmouth, Munchausen, and all the German faction,' &c.   Horace
Walpole, who faithfully reflected the paternal aversion to that 'faction,'
does his utmost to throw contempt upon Baron Münchhausen, and
ridicule upon his lady (*Letters*, vol. ii. p. 197; vol. iii. p. 114).

more or less critical significance for the affairs both of Great Britain and of the Electorate. In 1739 he was quarrelling with Denmark about Steinhorst, a fragment of the Duchy of Lauenburg, which he ultimately by Imperial mediation secured in return for a money payment. In 1731, 1732, 1741, and 1753, he contrived to effect additions (none of which were of special importance), either of a permanent or of a transitory sort, to his Electorate. The impulse which urged the King in this direction, and which seems to be an infirmity common to many crowned heads and great landowners, was censured and deplored by Münchhausen. For the rest, he was a historical conservative in his sentiments and sympathies ; and it is natural that in him these should have taken the political form of a conviction that, whatever mistakes Austria might commit, her action must be less detrimental than that of Prussia to the prospect of preserving the Empire. Thus he persisted in his preference of the cause which was conquered by reason of its intrinsic lack of reality rather than, even in the day of its waning fortunes, because of a dearth of high-minded champions. In Hanoverian politics he was hardly happier than in Imperial; for while he had at heart the security of the Electorate, for whose sake his prince had been so long accused of ignoring British interests, the inevitable had come to pass, even before he had reached the full height of his personal ascendancy, and the union between the two countries had, for the sake of the greater of them, entailed dire sufferings upon the less.

In so far as the interval between the War of the Austrian Succession and the Seven Years' War is to be regarded as leading up through divers vicissitudes to the epoch of the political supremacy of the elder Pitt, it may also be said to have prepared the downfall of the system of foreign policy dear to King George II and the Hanoverian interest represented by the Münchhausens. In the violent agitation of

the public mind which in the years 1756–7 was followed
by a public depression which pictured to itself the downfall
of England as a thing assured, the utter unpopularity of the
Crown, and the widespread conviction that the King had
conceived a deep hatred for his British subjects, counted for
much; so unimaginative a chronicler as Lord Waldegrave [1]
compares the situation with that which in 1641 had been
followed by the outbreak of the Civil War and the collapse
of the English monarchy.   More than this. When at the close
of this period of distraction Pitt at last took the helm, his
appointment may be said to have averted a personal contention between the Sovereign and the popular favourite on
the broad issue of the supposed undue leaning of the former
to the interests of his Electorate, and of the resistance to this
leaning, which in truth was as yet the chief foundation of Pitt's
popularity.   It was with so wonderful a rapidity to acquire
titles of a higher kind that one feels little disposed to enquire
whether, as something of tinsel had contributed to the glitter
of Pitt's earlier anti-Hanoverian speeches, so now there was
not something of inconsistency in his maintenance of the
subsidy system and the payment of Hanoverian troops.   He
had not invented these methods; and the undertakings into
which his active genius at once threw itself were too vast
and numerous to allow of his now devising others in their
place.   As for Hanover, to whatever use his ambition might
have hitherto put her needs or pretensions, his present task
was to make Great Britain's connexion with her serve as
best it could the purposes of the mighty struggle through
which he had undertaken to carry the nation.

However much against the wishes of King George II,
the second Silesian War had been brought to a close by
Great Britain's once more dissociating herself from ulterior

---

[1] *Memoirs*, p. 130.

undertakings on the part of Austria for the recovery of
Silesia. In the Peace of Aix-la-Chapelle the hated guarantee
of Silesia to Prussia had been renewed, and in Vienna the
question was already very directly raised whether it was
worth while to hold fast to the British alliance, which was fast
dwindling into a good understanding with the King rather than
with his Government. But Kaunitz's revolutionary proposal
of an alliance with France was at this time still rejected by
the Empress, and seems to have been temporarily abandoned
by its author in favour of the policy of a frank renunciation of
Silesia, which might have brought Prussia over into the alliance of Austria and the Maritime Powers. An excellent device
in the interests of the peace of Europe; but Kaunitz soon
found that his mistress would have none of it, and the traditions still cherished by George II and his Hanoverian advisers
(who, as might easily be shown, were about 1753 on as ill
terms as ever with Frederick II [1]) would have placed a serious
obstacle in the way of its acceptance by Great Britain. Thus
the British Government could only pursue its negotiations
in every possible quarter in view of the inevitable necessity
of resuming the war with France, of which, as we know, the
real issues lay outside the European complications. Other
Powers were approached with more or less success; our
engagements with Russia were regulated by a treaty, of which
the most important stipulation proved strangely ambiguous;
the United Provinces were pressed to take a more liberal
view of their obligations than accorded either with their
wishes or with their fears. But above all an understanding
was once more sought with Austria, and the negotiations at
Vienna reached their height in June, 1755. They were

[1] See the account of the negotiations with the Danish minister
Bernstorff (Johann Hartwig Ernst) carried on shortly before Newcastle,
on the death of his brother, succeeded him at the head of the Government (Havemann, vol. iii. p. 337).

conducted by Keith under instructions which in part proceeded jointly from Holdernesse as Secretary of State and
from Münchhausen—the Hanover Münchhausen, for the
King was once more in his electoral capital.   Thus, during
his last visit there the consequences of an identification of
British and Hanoverian policy were once more illustrated
with signal force.   Austria manifestly—Kaunitz said this in
so many words to Keith [1]—desired to consider the proposed
British alliance to be directed as much against Prussia as
against France.   Accordingly, a combination which should
seek to unite both these ends was sure to be attempted ; and
this was the meaning of the so-called Herrenhausen project
(June–July, 1755), elaborated by the Saxon minister Count
Fleming with Münchhausen and his Hanoverian colleague
Steinberg, with the approval of King George II.   It provided
for the signature of a treaty in which, as Elector of Hanover
(but of course with British subsidies in his hand), he should
agree with Austria and Saxony-Poland for the maintenance
of an army for the defence of Hanover, Saxony, and the
German dominions of the House of Austria, which with the
aid of an expected Russian diversion would enable the
Empress to send the desired 30,000 troops for the defence
of the Low Countries against France.   It was obvious, as
Holdernesse explained in a covering letter to Newcastle,
that the King's signature to such a treaty would imply
a promise of the requisite subsidies being furnished by
Great Britain ; it was equally obvious, as Newcastle perceived, that the Herrenhausen project made an appeal to
Parliament indispensable, and that this appeal would be
useless, if unsupported by Pitt as a responsible member of
the Cabinet.

[1] See Keith's letter to Newcastle, May 22, 1755, *ap.* Waddington,
Louis XV et le Renversement des Alliances, 1754-6 (Paris, 1896),
p. 134.

This was the very moment (July, 1755) when our American quarrels with France, followed by the seizure of French ships, had brought us to the actual brink of war with that Power, and the French Ambassador (the Duc de Mirepoix) had taken his departure from London. What could have been unhappier than that at such a time the belief should have been general which was afterwards expressed by Horace Walpole in the words : ' While Britain dared France, the monarch was trembling for his Hanover [1] ' ? Pitt, in the interview which, on behalf of the Cabinet, Lord Hardwicke had requested of him, declined co-operation on the basis of an indefinite extension of the subsidy system, such as must have ensued upon the adoption of the Herrenhausen project, which was accordingly doomed. But even had it been otherwise, and had the general detestation of the subsidy system not stood in the way, the Herrenhausen project—and this is why I have dwelt upon its collapse—would soon have revealed its fatal flaw. The Powers whom it designed to bind together more closely had quite different objects in view. Newcastle laid aside the project without any regret at having to consider the alternative which his master was so unwilling to face—a reconciliation with Prussia ; and by the beginning of August the negotiations with Austria may be said to have come to an end. The wrath of George II descended upon Lord Holdernesse ; and during the remainder of this troubled year he fell back upon the system of subsidy-treaties pure and simple, in order to be able to guard the Hanoverian frontier against all attacks, in this sense concluding a fresh agreement with Hesse-Cassel, and carrying on the negotiation with Russia. The agitation in Parliament against this detested system of treaties rose higher than ever : and Newcastle ventured upon one more appeal

---

[1] *Memoirs of the Last Ten Years of George II.* vol. ii. pp. 34–5.

to Pitt, in which the latter, though consenting to support
the Hessian treaty in which the King's honour was engaged,
refused to go further or identify himself with the system.
When the treaties came to be considered in Parliament
(December), Pitt's brother-in-law Temple moved in the
House of Lords for a censure, declaring that we were become
an insurance office to Hanover, and in the Commons Pitt
himself condemned them in more dignified, but not less
severe terms [1]. But Newcastle's hand was still on the main-
spring, and the Court prevailed.

The Austrian policy of the House of Hanover, which the
Pelham and Newcastle Governments had half-heartedly taken
over from Carteret, had broken down; and Great Britain
stood face to face with France, alone and to all appearance
dismayed. But this was not all. The negotiations between
Great Britain and Austria, of which the Herrenhausen project
may be regarded as the final phase, had come to an end
quite early in August; and before that month had closed,
the confidential negotiations between Austria and France had
begun. Their ultimate issue was, as you know, a revolution
in the relations between the chief European Powers so radical
as to wear the aspect of a dramatic surprise; but in truth it
was the reverse of unprepared and sudden. Its history, which
has been much obscured by partialities difficult in such a
connexion to repress, and by the rapid growth of legend in
an atmosphere of so much insincerity and concealment, has
been recently rewritten with rare clearness by M. Richard
Waddington, in a work cited in a previous note; but we
cannot concern ourselves with it here, except in so far as the
part played by Great Britain in these transactions illustrates
the final effort of Hanoverian policy to provide against what

---

[1] For an extremely interesting account of these debates, see *Memoirs
of the Last Ten Years of George II*, vol. ii. pp. 105–38.

had now become the plain issue of the Personal Union—viz. the danger in which Hanover was involved by it.   Probably few Englishmen would nowadays approve of Pitt's disdainful way of treating the risks to which British policy exposed Hanover.   The King, he said, would be certain to recover possession of his Electorate when the war was ended; if necessary let him then ask for an indemnity.

The Austrian negotiations, then, having failed, what were, during our struggle with France for colonial empire, likely to be our relations with our and Austria's former adversary, Hanover's hated neighbour King Frederick II of Prussia? As for that prince, though not apt to give way to sentiment in business hours, he had of late thought it advisable to show himself not absolutely indisposed to cultivate friendly relations with his uncle's Government.   As early as 1754 he had, with an instinctive perception, for which Carteret as protector of the ' Protestant interest ' would have found a grander name, shown himself willing to co-operate with the British and the Scandinavian Governments in the matter of the religious faith of the Hereditary Prince of Hesse-Cassel, who had become a convert to Rome.   In 1755, not long after the arrival of King George at Hanover, he had been prepared to pay a personal visit to his uncle,—a project which even the Hanoverian ministers did their best to promote, but which was defeated by the immoveable discourtesy of their master.   Of more significance was the visit to Hanover of his sister the Duchess Philippine Charlotte of Brunswick-Wolfenbüttel with her two daughters, the marriage of one of whom to George Prince of Wales was for a time encouraged by his grandfather[1].   For her husband, Duke Charles, was a prince

---

[1] The scheme fell through, as may be read in Horace Walpole, owing to the strong resistance offered to it by the Dowager Princess of Wales ; and the Princess Anna Amelia soon afterwards married the Hereditary Prince Ernest of Saxe-Weimar.   She was to become the tutelary

of considerable intelligence, and very distinctly contributed
to the establishment of friendlier relations between the Prussian
and Hanoverian Courts.   During her visit King George II
spoke to her in a reassuring tone of his intention to prevent
any attack upon his Electorate, and of subsidising troops of
her husband's for the purpose ; and she apprised Münchhausen of this conversation.   Upon this hint, it seems that the
British statesmen still charged with the conduct of our foreign
policy began to familiarise both themselves and the King
with the idea of an arrangement with Prussia, as a *pis-aller*
for a satisfactory alliance with Austria ; and Münchhausen
may be supposed to have fallen in with this change of face,
because he had the Brunswick marriage scheme more immediately in his mind.   But manifestly the security of the
Electorate was the ultimate purpose which British · and
Hanoverian statesmanship alike had in view; and for
which, in default of an Austrian alliance, an understanding with Prussia now seemed indispensable.   Thus,
covering this ulterior design by the Brunswick marriage-
negotiation, Münchhausen at last ventured on a note which
is still extant in Frederick the Great's Correspondence, and
which requested the good offices of the Duke and Duchess
for obtaining from the King of Prussia an undertaking of
neutrality, should Hanover be attacked by a French army.
Here, then, we have the germ of an alliance which was to
shake the world.   The Duke of Brunswick, who could
hardly foresee how closely the consequences of his action
were to tie the fortunes of his own house to those of Great
Britain, leading it from the glory of Minden to the tragedy
of Quatrebras, in the end yielded to the personal pressure

spirit of the dawn of a great age of German literature. It would be
idle to speculate as to the influence she might have exercised over the
progress of our own, had she been actually united to the future King
George III.

N

of Holdernesse, and communicated to Berlin (September 2)
the British proposal that Prussia would remain neutral in
the event of a French attack upon Hanover, and should even
endeavour to prevent such an attack.   No difficulty, it was
added, could exist as to a suitable equivalent, should King
Frederick assent.   Although Frederick's reply to the Duke
of Brunswick was quite vague, while in the accompanying
private letter he characteristically declined to commit himself, and showed a perfect insight into the situation, he at
once began to make enquiries in London; and Dutch and
English journals promptly announced that he had agreed
to a treaty of neutrality in return for a round sum.   As
a matter of fact, he was still hesitating.   Once more,
through the Duke of Brunswick, he apprised the British
Government that his treaty of alliance with France would
expire early in the coming year; that he would then be
free to act; but that the first proposals could not come
from him.   At the same time he sent word to Versailles that
he desired to see at Potsdam the Duc de Nivernais,
a highly accomplished statesman to whom he was particularly attached, in order to communicate to him certain
overtures recently received.   While the French Government
committed the irrevocable fault of allowing Nivernais to
delay his departure for four months, till it was too late, the
British risked spoiling its game by playing it too openly.
Holdernesse eagerly proposed to settle the matter by sending
a confidential envoy to Berlin to bring it to a conclusion
under the King's own eyes.   Frederick, maintaining the
character of a present ally of France, who had shown herself
most obliging in the affair of East Frisia, replied that if he
were to sacrifice his preferences, his hatreds, his personal
feelings and passions, it would be indispensable that the
interests of Prussia should coincide with those of the Power
which made proposals to him.   And, by way of emphasis, he

added privately that he could not be expected in reason to turn France out of doors, in order to have the satisfaction of preserving to the English this country of Hanover, for which he for his part cared neither the one way nor the other. Notwithstanding this confident tone, he was however very anxious as to the English negotiations with Russia, and the existing treaty between those two Powers. Dissatisfied with the vagueness of the British reply (of November 21), he instructed Knyphausen at Paris to protest against the malicious insinuations afloat as to his having entered into an engagement with Great Britain; but a few days later he began his negotiations with her in earnest, by entrusting the conduct of them to Abraham Ludwig Michell, the Prussian Secretary of Legation in London. This skilful diplomatist quickly contrived to obtain through Henry Fox, now Secretary of State in the place of Robinson, copies of the Russian treaty with Great Britain, and of the British proposals for an understanding with Prussia. On finding that a treaty of neutrality would include a renewal of the Silesian guarantee, a removal of apprehensions of Russian intervention, and a fair settlement of the difficulty as to the Prussian ships seized during the last war, Frederick perceived that these were the conditions which he wanted; and without further hesitation set about securing them. Nine days after Michell's letter was written, Frederick signified his acceptance (December 7), and certain final difficulties having been removed, and a judicious alteration in the wording adopted [1], the treaty, which is sometimes oddly enough called the Second Treaty of Westminster, was signed at Whitehall on January 16, 1756. The two Powers expressed their common desire to maintain

---

[1] In the neutrality stipulation, the term 'Germany' was substituted for 'Germanic Empire,' so as to exclude the Austrian Netherlands; but the former seems actually to have been the term suggested in Frederick's first letter.

peace in Germany ; they agreed to oppose the entrance into or passage through it of any foreign army, and each renewed the guarantee of the possessions of the other.

The full significance of the Anglo-Prussian neutrality treaty was not contained within its four corners or present to the minds of those who were concerned in bringing it to a conclusion,—not even to the mind of Frederick the Great himself.   King George II rejoiced; as Horace Walpole says[1], 'this guarantee of Germany, this thorn drawn out of the side of Hanover, dispelled at once his aversion to his nephew.' The British ministers were troubled by doubts, Newcastle in particular, and these doubts were echoed by Münchhausen. It was indisputably well that short work should have been made of the preposterous interpretation of the clause in the Anglo-Russian treaty, binding each Power to communicate to the other any negotiation concerning the *common enemy*, by which term, according to the Russians, the King of Prussia was signified.   Above all, it was well that the treaty should have followed with such speed upon the rejection of the French *ultimatum* by the British ministry, which made war with France inevitable.   Yet it remained surprising that Frederick II, who could not be desirous of throwing down the gauntlet to France, should have ventured to keep her in the dark, at the very time when her special envoy the Duc de Nivernais was at last arriving in Berlin.   But neither could Frederick know the extent of the risk which he had run by his extraordinary rapidity of action, nor was the British nation aware of the prospect that was opening for its future by a compact which for the first time placed it and the Prussian King side by side.   Nor, in fine, could King George and the Hanoverians anticipate what vicissitudes this connexion was to bring upon the Electorate, in whose interest they had

---

[1] *Memoirs of the Last Ten Years of George II*, vol. ii. p. 152.

assented to it, at first with so much reluctance and even now
not without misgivings. For none of them had in their hands
the true key to the situation—a knowledge of the negotiations
which had during the last few months been in progress
between Austria and France. Whether but for the conclusion
of the Anglo-Prussian agreement these negotiations would
have ended as they did—in a compact which, like that of
Westminster itself, was not a treaty of offensive alliance, but
which was to develope into a league of partition (May, 1757)
—may perhaps be open to doubt. We have the positive
assertion to the contrary of the Abbé de Bernis, upon whom
the chief responsibility on the French side rests. Yet now
that these transactions have at last been placed comprehen-
sively and lucidly before us, the conclusion has become
almost irresistible, that it was the action of Frederick II in
agreeing to the British treaty which stung the supine and
pacifically disposed Government of Louis XV into taking the
first step that made the second inevitable. If this was so,
then the anxiety of King George II, and of those who thought
with him to safeguard the Hanoverian frontier, was the final
cause of the Franco-Austrian agreement, which so largely
influenced the course, and determined the character, of the
Seven Years' War.

LECTURE VI

KLOSTER ZEVEN AND SUHLINGEN

THE British ministry had for a season flattered itself
that the Treaty of Westminster, upon which it looked
with very half-hearted satisfaction as upon an arrangement
for the protection of the Hanoverian Electorate—an object
with which it was not easy to captivate a Parliament and
people dejected as to the condition of their own affairs—
meant no more than this. It would, so they were content
to suppose, leave the ancient system of alliances unaltered;
Austria and the United Provinces remaining unestranged;
and the Russian alliance, which dated from 1742, being
renewed by means of the treaty which Sir Charles Hanbury
Williams had brought to pass with more pains than skill.
Indeed, Münchhausen seems to have thought that Fleming's
stillborn scheme of an alliance between Austria, Saxony-
Poland, and England, which had attracted him so greatly,
might still be saved from its ashes, or indeed extended by the
inclusion of Prussia, now in so pliable a mood, and that all
might yet be well. So blind is the fondness of politicians
for proposals which they have made their own, that they
seem at times incapable of perceiving such schemes to have
been materially altered by a process which to blunter wits
seems like turning them inside out. As for the factors in
Münchhausen's revived project, you know how Saxony was,
before the year was out, to fare at the hands of the ally he
was proposing for her. The new Anglo-Russian treaty,

which had been concluded by Great Britain largely in deference to the wishes of Austria, became a dead letter in consequence of the Treaty of Westminster; for Great Britain
could not now use it against Prussia, the sole *ennemi commun*
against whom the Czarina Elizabeth wished her troops to be
employed. Hence no troops were forthcoming, and no
subsidies were paid; but you will look in vain among the
facetious effusions of Sir Charles Hanbury Williams' muse
for any verses on a theme of much satirical promise.

A more seductive offer, as holding out a prospect of
safety on both sides, was that which appears to have been
in June, 1756, insinuated through Lady Yarmouth by the
Danish minister in London, Count Rantzau, who drew his
inspiration from Paris as well as from Vienna. This took
the shape of a scheme of neutrality based on an agreement
with Austria, to whom or to one of whose allies Hameln—
situate, as we all know, on the river Weser in the principality
of Calenberg—was to be delivered up as a pledge. The
plan was very honourably rejected by George II before it
had come to the knowledge either of the British Cabinet or
of the Prussian King. But it seems certain that this clandestine transaction was encouraged by Kaunitz, besides being
apparently known to the French Government; and, as will be
seen, the echoes of it had not quite died out in the following
year [1].

I spoke just now of satire; but something far different
from ridicule would be an appropriate *envoi* to a contrast
between the events that followed upon the Treaty of Westminster and the intentions with which it had been concluded.
When Frederick II had accepted it in principle with a rapidity
bordering on rashness, his chief motive cannot but have been
to place a serious if not insuperable obstacle in the way of

[1] As to this scheme, see *Memoirs of the Last Ten Years of George II*,
vol. iii. p. 12 and note.

an eventual Russian attack upon his dominions, such as would
have well suited Austria.   Yet it was an offensive combination between these two Powers, which after giving him great
trouble in the third year of the war, in the fourth (1752)
brought him near to despairing of his destiny.   The British
Government's primary motive in settling the treaty had been
the protection of the electoral dominions of the King, whose
solicitude for their safety had hitherto so far exceeded that
manifested by his Parliament.   But even before, in consequence of the French descent upon Minorca, war had been
actually declared against France, the fear of invasion had led
to a proposal (April 29, 1756) for the despatch of the electoral troops to England for the defence of these coasts.   Pitt
opposed the motion in a speech which really struck at the
root of the illogical and yet inevitable consequences of the
Personal Union which it aimed at utilising.   Not only—
which was the less evil—was the proposal one which dictated
to the Elector how to dispose of his soldiery; but—and
herein lay its moral obliquity—by baring the Electorate of
troops for the sake of England, we placed another country in
a situation of immediate danger, simply because it happened
to be under the rule of our King.   The motion was carried
by an overwhelming majority, and during the summer the
Hanoverians were encamped near Maidstone [1].   Then, however, came early in 1757 the real stress of the German war.
Pitt, whom the King had blamed for unwillingness to do his
business—and as Granville said to Fox, it was known what
this business was [2]—brought down a royal message asking

[1] Ballantyne, p. 345, from Horace Walpole.
[2] At the end of 1756 they were sent back with a broad hint that their
services would not again be required, in the shape of the recommenda-
tion of the scheme of a national militia in the King's speech.   George II
did not like this proposal, which was thrown out in 1756, but carried in
1757.   See Stanhope, vol. iv. p. 86, and cf. Hallam (10th ed.), vol. iii.
p. 262.

for a grant of £200,000 in defence of the Electorate ; and
this vote was merely the precursor of an expenditure without
precedent or parallel for the same purpose on the part of both
King and country.   Yet what were the results which ultimately remained with the Electorate and the electoral family ?
A collapse, on which it is difficult to look back without a
sense of shame, involved in its discredit the one member
of that family whom either King George or the English people
had at any time regarded with pride ; nor had the King himself been able wholly to cast off his share of responsibility for
what had come to pass.   And as for the Electorate, it underwent privations and sufferings, such as had not befallen it
since the days of the Thirty Years' War.

After the death of George II, and at a time following
shortly upon the resignation of Pitt, a clever but reckless
speaker was put forward in the House of Commons (into
which he would appear to have been brought for the purpose),
to vilify the statesman who had never been greater than in his
fall.   On one of these occasions Colonel Barré, defiant of calls
to order, opened his attack by asserting that during the late
reign everything was made subservient to Hanoverian counsels and interests ; the present King, he added with perhaps
too much point, had never looked on a map of Hanover[1].
No one honestly believed or believes that the blood and
treasure expended by Great Britain during the struggle of
the Seven Years' War, even in so far as it was expended on
German soil, is to be placed to the account of the sorely-tried
Electorate.   But the *animus* against Hanover, which survived
to the latter days of the war, was still very rife in the earlier,
when to the widespread disfavour provoked by the King's
known personal sympathies was united a more or less well-
founded suspicion of the continued activity of his electoral

[1] Horace Walpole, *Memoirs of the Reign of George III* (ed. 1894),
vol. i. p. 86.

counsellors. It would be an error to suppose that either he or they, with the brothers Münchhausen prominent among them, had the least intention of making use of the Treaty of Westminster as a first step towards the establishment of a solidarity of interests, or that they contemplated with satisfaction or acquiescence the event of Hanover being without any further safeguard exposed to the chances of a British war. Hence, at the outset of the struggle, a vacillation to which nothing short of events of unprecedented magnitude could have set a term.

The army which early in 1757 was, with the aid of subsidy-treaties and the grant proposed by Pitt, collected for the defence of the Electorate, contained, in addition to the Hanoverians born, Brunswickers, Hessians, and Gothaers, but no British soldier, with the exception of its commander-in-chief. The Duke of Cumberland arrived in Hanover at the close of April, after in the beginning of the month the French army under Marshal d'Estrées had crossed the Rhine. Westphalia was occupied, and whatever assurances might have been transmitted to Hanover by the Marshal, it was to become more and more manifest that the Electorate was directly threatened. Even now the negotiations as to a Hanoverian neutrality were not at an end, and Count Colloredo, the Austrian ambassador in London, suggested a scheme of treaty which would have opened a *transitus innoxius* to the Empress and her allies through the greater part of the Electorate. No answer had been given to this proposal on the part of the King-Elector, when on May 1 the secret treaty of offensive alliance (the so-called Partition Treaty) between France and Austria was signed at Versailles.

I am obliged to restrict myself to a single word on the significance of the appointment of the Duke of Cumberland, and the nature of the authority which it conferred on him. The Duke of Cumberland was a personage whose public

importance remained little diminished, even when the cruelties
that had followed upon his victory of Culloden, and for which
he must in part be held responsible, had put an end to his
widespread popularity. He continued to assert himself as
a high military authority, and by the public at large, then
still very incurious in such matters, he was readily accepted at
his word. For political business he entertained and expressed
a lofty contempt; and though not devoid of shrewdness,
he had not allowed himself to be disturbed in his inherited
notions by the flow of accumulated wisdom which old Horace
Walpole had directed to his special address, concerning the
advantages of a thorough co-operation with Prussia. What
he liked in public men was frank servility; and no doubt
he was not always left ungratified. To Pitt he had an
utter aversion. Frederick II cannot be said to have judged
unwisely, when, after one or two other suggestions which had
proved impracticable, he expressed a wish that the Duke of
Cumberland should be appointed to the command of the
electoral army. For it was clearly in Prussia's interest that
this command should be in the hands of some personage
with authority to overawe the Hanoverian Government, which
was still at the last moment endeavouring to impress its wish
for neutrality upon the King through the younger Münchhausen. In point of fact a measure of authority was
accorded to the Duke in Hanover, which is almost[1] *sui
generis* in the history of the Personal Union, and which we
shall probably not be wrong in connecting with King George II's
long-continued wish (of which some traces appear to exist
in this very year 1757) for an ultimate dissolution of that
connexion. Before Cumberland left England his parting
admonition to his father had urged the dismissal of Pitt.

---

[1] At least before the appointments of the Duke of Cambridge as
Military Governor in 1813, as Governor-General in 1816, and as
Viceroy (with materially enlarged powers) in 1831.

As you know, the advice was actually carried out, and Pitt quitted office in April, not resuming it till late in June.   More keen-eyed than either sire or son, Frederick II transmitted assurances to the dismissed statesman of his continued regard. He at least hoped to make the Hanoverian army what it ultimately became—an active factor in his plan of operations.

But the way to a share in the laurels of the Great War lay through the Caudine Forks.   The news of Frederick's great victory of Prague (May 6), which first aroused the feeling of enthusiasm for him in England which was afterwards to swell to so vast a volume, enabled the King to censure Colloredo with that contemptuous discourtesy of which, under all circumstances, he was so perfect a master; and with equally characteristic frugality he lost no time in requesting the victor to despatch reinforcements to the Duke of Cumberland.   But the very next courier brought the disheartening tidings that the Prussian arms had suffered the great reverse of Kolin (June 18), which made the evacuation of Bohemia indispensable, and thus brought to a complete collapse the bold offensive movement with which Frederick had opened the war.

I do not wish to discuss from any point of view but one the circumstances of the catastrophe that followed, and that went further than any other transaction belonging to the history of the Personal Union, and in itself due to the circumstances of that Union, towards leaving a stain upon our national honour.   For in a monarchy, whether constitutional or other, the honour of the Sovereign is the honour of the nation; nor can it in candour be denied that the British ministry was cognisant of the real nature of the action of King George II in the matter of the Convention of Kloster Zeven.   The facts of the case are perfectly patent from the *Newcastle Papers*, and are, with the aid of these, exposed only too clearly by M. Richard Waddington in his new volume.   The consciousness of what had actually taken place was, no doubt, readily thrust aside under the transcendent effect of the great achievements which filled the years next ensuing; but the truth was not wholly ignored at the time, and now stands forth with the utmost distinctness.

Cumberland's army was efficiently drilled, and composed of troops accustomed to act together; but it was little more than half of the French forces in numbers. Indifferently commanded, therefore, though the French were before the battle, and (as it seems scarcely too much to say) ill commanded though they were after it, one may concede that they could scarcely have been permanently prevented by so much weaker an adversary from making their way into the Electorate. But it seems equally fair to assume that it was in Cumberland's power to give them serious trouble, and by averting so rapid and complete an occupation of the Electorate as was actually effected, to respond in some measure to the purpose with which he had been sent forth. The line of the Rhine had never been defended; and he was probably right in regarding the line of the Weser as untenable. But what can be urged in explanation or in palliation of his actual course? After (to put it in a few words) collecting his forces on the home side of the Weser at the one end of the Electorate, he gave battle, and then, having lost the day by his own precipitancy in accepting defeat, when victory was within his grasp, he retreated to the other end. His object, of course, was to gain a position whence he could cover Stade, and thus keep open his communications with England; and he afterwards, no doubt correctly, reminded the King his father that his original instructions and the ensuing correspondence had been based upon the plan of operations which he actually pursued, and that an eventual retreat upon Magdeburg had never been taken into consideration. As a matter of fact, the suggestion by the British Cabinet, inspired by the King of Prussia, of a retreat in this

direction was first made just a week *after* the Convention of
Kloster Zeven had been signed. To the plan laid down
for him, Cumberland, with characteristic obstinacy, adhered,
thereby at first actually bewildering his adversary Richelieu,
who could not but think that reinforcements would arrive from
England, and then obliging the unwilling French commander
to follow in his footsteps. The territory of Hesse-Cassel had
been left open to the enemy before the battle of Hastenbeck;
and through it a second French army, in conjunction with the
troops of the Empire, could now advance upon Thuringia
and Saxony. As for the Hanoverian Electorate, after Hastenbeck had been fought and lost (July 26), it fell an easy
prey to the foe, and on August 10 Richelieu entered the
capital; while the Duke of Brunswick concluded a treaty
with the French, who occupied the whole of his dominions,
except a corner left to him for residence; and when on September 3 the French had surprised Harburg, the Duke of
Cumberland and his army of defence were completely isolated
on the strip of territory between Elbe and Oste, with the
fortress of Stade, where the Hanoverian Privy Council had
taken refuge, in their rear. Five days afterwards the Duke
signed the Convention of Kloster Zeven, in which Denmark
by Richelieu's request had acted as mediatress, and which, as
you know, provided that Cumberland should dismiss his
auxiliaries, while the Hanoverians should be distributed in
cantonments on the right bank of the Elbe, with a garrison
at Stade, and the French should remain in occupation of the
Electorate at large.

We need not enter into the question as to the judgment, or
the want of judgment, shown by Richelieu in concluding the
Convention of Kloster Zeven, which at the time was disapproved in principle by the Government of Louis XV, and
would probably have been visited severely on the head of
a commander less in favour at Court, and which was after-

wards censured by Napoleon as an act of inexplicable folly. Our concern is rather with Cumberland's acceptance of the agreement, and with the view taken of this step in Hanover and in England. As for Hanover, the Electorate was in the grasp of the enemy; and it seems quite explicable, that inasmuch as nothing could be so calamitous for the country as a continuance of active hostilities, the news of the convention should there have caused a general feeling of relief, the solitary voice raised in deprecation of so sudden a self-immolation being that of the most prominent member of the Government, Münchhausen[1]. In England, on the other hand, where no actual consequences of the agreement could except remotely be in question, it produced extreme indignation; and the Duke of Cumberland had become so unpopular that there was nothing to interfere with the unanimity with which he was made responsible for the catastrophe. More surprising was the circumstance that the loudest and the harshest condemnation of the Duke of Cumberland's conduct proceeded from the Elector-King, his father.

The personal aspect of this incident has but a faint interest for a later age. Certain it is that in the public career of the Duke of Cumberland nothing became him so well as the self-restraint which dignified its close. But the final refusal of King George II to ratify the Convention of Kloster Zeven is an incident of great significance, both for the history of the Personal Union and for that of the Great War, in which the two countries connected by it were engaged. For, in a word, it involved a decision on the part of the King to enter into the policy of active co-operation with Prussia, now distinctly adopted by Pitt, and it put an end to the attempt to pursue a Hanoverian programme or

---

[1] Horace Walpole says that the London Münchhausen was ' the most indecent ' of all who indulged in personal invectives against the Duke. *Memoirs of the Last Ten Years of George II*, vol. iii. p. 60.

system of action side by side with a British. Unhappily, however, this repudiation was not on the part of George II an
act of good faith, and the leading members of the British
ministry, though unaware of the extent of his engagements,
were not ignorant of the original intentions of which the
repudiation implied the disavowal. Very briefly put, the order
of events had been something as follows. After Hastenbeck
a suggestion had been made in the British Cabinet to
despatch, in aid of Cumberland, a force of 9,000 men then
n readiness at Chatham, and Richelieu, as already noted, had
been apprehensive of such a step being taken ; but, chiefly in
deference to Pitt, who thought that the force might be more
effectively employed elsewhere, the notion had been dropped.
The King had accordingly continued his efforts for securing
either the neutrality of Hanover, or a separate peace between
her and France, carrying on negotiations in this sense at
Vienna, at Copenhagen, and directly through Münchhausen
with Marshal d'Estrées, then still in command of the French
invading army. The British Cabinet was quite aware of what
was in progress, and Newcastle gave vent to his fears of the
impression that would be made upon the King of Prussia by
such an abandonment of his alliance. But formally the business
was an electoral concern, and even when on August 10 King
George communicated to Newcastle a further letter received
from his son, announcing that the Hanoverians were in full
retreat upon Stade and in a desperate condition, the ministers
left the King to decide for himself. His decision was taken
on the following day (August 11), when he transmitted to
the Duke of Cumberland a series of documents too long
to be described here, but culminating, if I may so say, in
a letter in which the King gives it as his opinion that nothing
remains but to negotiate with the French commander (now
Richelieu) 'a separate peace, or a neutrality, or even a preliminary arrangement, as speedily and on as favourable terms

as possible, for the relief of the country and the preservation of the army.' Full powers to the above effect were enclosed to Cumberland under the same date ; and it is to these, which are textually extant, that Pitt referred when he replied to the King's assertion that he had given his son no orders to conclude : ' But full powers, sir,—very full powers[1].' A better witness still, however, on this head has been summoned by M. Waddington. In the British Museum[2] may be seen the original draft by Lord Holdernesse, disapproving of the despatch sent to the Duke on receipt of the untoward news. In this draft the King has with his own hand crossed out certain words charging the Duke with having signed the convention ' upon conditions which His Majesty has been pleased to declare to me your Royal Highness was not authorised to accept,' and has added the marginal comment : ' He had a full power, and this part must be alter'd.' Newcastle's hand has accordingly made the necessary alteration ; so that the letter goes on at once to express the King's surprise that the convention should have been carried into execution by the Duke without waiting for the royal ratification.

At the time these instructions were not communicated by the King to his ministers ; and though of the general drift of his intentions they were fully aware, both from his own hints, and through Lady Yarmouth and the London Münchhausen, they may, I think, be acquitted of any knowledge before the fact as to the powers given by the King to the Duke. Of Frederick's views with regard to a treaty of neutrality or a separate peace they were soon made cognisant ; but before they were informed of these they induced the King to suggest

[1] Horace Walpole, in the passage cited in the last note. The same authority asserts that George II told the Spanish Ambassador that he had written to his son, positively commanding him to fight ; but that the letter, though written, was never sent.

[2] *Additional MSS.*, 32,874, p. 163.

to Cumberland a retreat upon Magdeburg,—the Kloster Zeven
Convention having, as I have said, been already signed.

It is therefore clear, both that the British ministry did
nothing to stop or modify the King's action, and that this
action was such as to make the King responsible for Cumberland's signature of the convention.   If, notwithstanding,
his wrath blazed up against his unlucky son from the moment
of the arrival of the news, we cannot in fairness attribute this
result merely to the vacillation not unnatural in a passionate
prince of seventy-five years of age.   The convention, which
left nearly the whole of the Electorate in the hands of the
enemy, had certainly, as M. Waddington points out, 'relieved'
it after a fashion which could scarcely have been contemplated
by the Elector.   Such, however, as the convention was, how
could it now be dealt with, in view of the authorisation conveyed in the King's own instructions, the remonstrances of the
King of Prussia, and the indignation of the British people?

To the ministry, the exigencies of the situation seemed
to be adequately met by a declaration affirming that the
Government had had no share in the convention, and that
it would in no wise affect the action of Great Britain.   But
they can hardly be said to have by this simple expedient
succeeded in dissociating themselves from the antecedents of
the transaction.   For the moment discouragement prevailed,
but soon the arrival of better news from Germany exercised
its effect, and if the King should resolve to repudiate the
convention, he would be sure of being met halfway by his
British ministers, among whom, as a matter of course, Pitt
took the lead in advocating a forward policy.   The King's
difficulty as to repudiation was twofold.   In the first place,
a pretext must be found; but this, of course, might be
managed.   For while there could be no question of a modification of the agreement going so far as to provide for
the evacuation by the French of the whole of the Electorate,

or of the greater part of it, the convention had been hastily
and carelessly drawn up, and advantage might be taken of
some oversight or omission.   But if, as was supposed, the
dislocation of Cumberland's army had already begun, a de-
nunciation of the convention would have placed the scattered
troops at the mercy of the enemy.   By a stroke of good luck
it proved that a difficulty about disarming the Hessians
before their return home had delayed the dispersion of
Cumberland's army, and that this hitch could be made a
pretext for either breaking off the entire agreement or at
least delaying its execution.   By the time of Cumberland's
return to England, the King was clearly intent upon repudiation.   But it was resolved this time to avoid precipitancy ; for
there might any day arrive the news of a Prussian victory,
when, if the convention had not yet been openly denounced,
an excellent opportunity would be afforded for an unexpected
attack upon the French army now occupying the Electorate.

The British ministry was encouraged by its knowledge
of these speculations to go a step further, and at a meeting of
a committee of the Cabinet held early in October, at which
the London Münchhausen was present, Pitt drew up a resolution which, while continuing to deprecate any interference
with the King's electoral possessions, expressed the opinion
of the British ministers that in the event of the repudiation of
the convention the electoral army should be taken into
British pay.   Although, even after this, the King seems to
have thought it well not absolutely to drop all proposals for
negotiating a satisfactory separate understanding between
the Electorate and France, his resolution was fast ripening
in a contrary direction.   He was untouched by the continued
protests of his Hanoverian Privy Council against a proceeding which would expose the Electorate to the vengeance of
the French forces ; but he appears to have been unable to
suppress a fear as to what might be the consequences of such

a step if the King of Prussia should be found to have treated on his own account with the French, or if—worse still—he should be defeated by them in battle.   Accordingly, as a last resort, he commissioned the London Münchhausen to undertake a winter's journey to Stade, in order to report on the situation. But its issue was to be decided for him neither by the fears of his Hanoverian Privy Council for the fate of the Electorate, nor by the lofty disregard of Pitt and his colleagues for so secondary a consideration.   On November 5 Frederick the Great gained the victory of Rossbach, which raised popular enthusiasm in England on behalf of our ally to its full height, and opened to Hanover a prospect of speedy liberation from the presence of the foe.   The Convention of Kloster Zeven was no longer worth the paper on which the agreement signed by a British prince, with full powers from his Sovereign, had been written; in his place his kinsman Prince Ferdinand of Brunswick, one of King Frederick's most trusted generals, was appointed commander of the electoral army; by the end of March, 1758, the Electorate was entirely freed from the French occupation; and in the following month Pitt, who earlier in the year had without a dissentient voice obtained the grant of an enormous Prussian subsidy, carried a further vote for taking the electoral army into British pay.   Finally, Prince Ferdinand's victory at Crefeld (June) induced Pitt to take the step to which he had refused his assent before Hastenbeck, and a body of British troops (8,000) was despatched to the Prince's aid.   Thus, at an advanced stage of the war, comradeship in arms at last effectually linked together those British and Hanoverian interests which at the commencement of the struggle had been so carefully and persistently kept asunder.   The military genius of Prince Ferdinand, which succeeded in assimilating the heterogeneous elements of which his army was composed, was able simultaneously to add to the great achievements of an alliance of vital importance for the future of Great Britain and her Empire, and to protect the Electorate. After he had liberated the whole of the Hanoverian and Brunswick dominions, together with the Hessian, seized by the French as the first prize of Cumberland's dilatory strategy, the greater part of the Electorate was, during the later years of the war, spared the burden and suffering of further invasion. Only the southern-most portions of its territories, including the towns of Münden and Göttingen, were from time to time in French hands; in the latter the professors, quite in the spirit of the eighteenth century, regularly carried on their courses before a diminished auditory. In 1761 a second French invasion was planned with the design of reconquering the whole of the Hanover-Brunswick lands, but the action of the combined French armies of Soubise and Broglie was crippled by Prince Ferdinand's victory of Vellinghausen (July, 1761); and in the following year a series of brilliant operations crowned the success of his plan of defence. Yet the sacrifices entailed upon the Electorate, and upon the adjoining Duchy of Brunswick, had been extremely heavy, and their sufferings during the months of entire occupation after Hastenbeck intense; though Richelieu's soldiery probably did him an injustice in claiming him as an associate in the license which he tolerated, and popular rumour seems to have erred in supposing the splendours of his Parisian hotel to have been due to the spoils of his northern campaign.

That the few years of a war carried on conjointly, and of sacrifices made in different ways for what had become a common purpose, had not sufficed to impart a permanent consistency to the tie uniting Great Britain and the German dominions of her Sovereign, was once more made manifest by the pacification that ended the struggle. When, under cir-cumstances and influences which cannot here be considered, peace with France was concluded by Great Britain under her new King, on her own account and without consideration for her Prussian ally, what thought was taken by her of her Hanoverian dependency—for such the Electorate had, for the purposes of the war, practically become? In the Preliminaries a clause had originally been proposed, stipulating for the restitution of German territories (viz. Hanover, Brunswick, and Hesse-Cassel) in the condition in which the first French invasion had found them. But this clause was subsequently withdrawn, and another substituted requiring only as speedy as possible an evacuation of these territories. Thus it was previously to the definitive signature of the Treaty of Peace that the British troops in the army commanded by Prince Ferdinand took their departure for Holland; and before the close of the year 1762 he resigned his command[1]. The impression left by the Peace of Paris upon the Power who had been our ally during four years of unparalleled eventfulness, but whose interests it had now suited the British Government entirely to ignore, was not likely to be transitory; and to Hanover, as a matter of course, the effects of this impression were at a later date, and in more than one passage of the later history of the Personal Union, to become of very great moment indeed.

In lieu of the brief outline which I had proposed to give of the relations between Hanover and Great Britain during the latter half of that history, from the close of the Seven Years' War onwards, I must, however, content myself with a few detached references, and cannot try to cover even that part of the ground on whose significance for the history of British as well as Hanoverian policy I just now touched. These references may, however, serve to show how much there is to invite enquiry in this portion also of a theme which I could not in the nature of the case hope to exhaust on the present occasion.

[1] Heinemann, vol. iii. p. 285.

During the earlier years of the long reign of George III
his Electorate was an object of comparatively little interest to
British politicians, although it was not overlooked by them so
entirely as might be supposed by students absorbed in the great
colonial and maritime issues of this period of our history.   In
Hanover, the continuous connexion with Great Britain was not
merely an incidental source of a harmless kind of pride which
might without offence be classed as provincial patriotism, and
from which even the serene academic atmosphere of Göttingen
derived a pleasant accession of self-consciousness, but it was
also productive of certain negative consequences of more solid
importance.   In the absence of the Sovereign, affairs were
conducted by the Privy Council, composed exclusively of
members of the higher native nobility.   Their methods of
government, however slow in rate of motion, were in perfect
harmony with the eminently conservative ways of thought and
life of the Lower-Saxon population ; the taxes were not
burdensome, and were increased neither by the residence of a
Court nor by the pressure of an officiously busy foreign policy.

On the other hand, King George III, while undoubtedly
interested in the general prosperity of his German dominions,
was not by education or habits of mind careful to distinguish
between British and Hanoverian political purposes ; it was
simpler, when they came into contact, to let the former include
the latter.   The elder Münchhausen, who survived to 1770,
in his last years largely confined his special attention to those
educational matters which were perhaps nearest to his heart ;
and neither he nor his successor Christian von Behr can have
desired that Hanover should play a prominent part in the
politics of the Empire.   After Great Britain's abandonment
of Prussia in the Peace of Paris, it was impossible that the
relations between the two Powers should be cordial ; and it
must be allowed that in the policy of the great King during
the later years of his reign there was little to commend it to

British interests or sympathies. In the War of the Bavarian
Succession (1778–9), carried on at a time when Great Britain
was at the height of her struggle against her American
Colonies, whose side France and Spain in these years successively joined, Hanover remained neutral, inclining rather
to the Austrian side. In the important transactions, however,
connected with the last achievement of Frederick the
Great, the establishment of the *Fürstenbund* (1785), which,
while checkmating Joseph II's design of exchanging the
Austrian Netherlands for Bavaria, formed an unmistakeable
step towards the disintegration of the old Empire, Hanoverian diplomacy co-operated with Prussian, and was supported by British statesmanship in the person of Sir James
Harris (afterwards Earl of Malmesbury[1]). The motive of his
action was beyond doubt a desire to establish intimate relations between Prussia and Great Britain, who was left in
isolation even after she had made peace with her many
adversaries. Thus, curiously enough, British interests were
once more paramount in determining the accession of
Hanover to a policy which could not otherwise than detri-
mentally affect the cohesion of the Empire, the liberty of
whose princes it proposed to safeguard. The disloyalty
towards that Empire of the policy of Joseph II avenged itself
indirectly as well as directly upon the House of Austria, whose

[1] A very active part was played in these transactions by Hardenberg,
who, as mentioned above, missed only by accident being appointed
Hanoverian minister in London, and thus lost any opportunity of inter-
vening directly—who can say to what purposes?—in the unfortunate
complications that followed on the Peace of Bâle. As minister of the
Duke of Brunswick, he was active in furthering the inclusion of both
Brunswick and Hanover in the *Fürstenbund*; and it is noteworthy to
find in co-operation with him a British Prince, the Duke of York, who as
Bishop of Osnabrück resided for some years at Hanover, while three of
his brothers (the Dukes of Cumberland, Sussex, and Cambridge) studied
at Göttingen.

interests he had so logically at heart ; and by a remarkable
chain of consequences the House of Hanover, which even
the course of the Seven Years' War had not altogether
alienated from its traditional sympathies, actively contributed
to advance this stage of the dissolving process.   Indeed,
the Hanoverian minister Beulwitz, whom Ranke[1] states to
have been previously active as Hanoverian envoy at Ratisbon,
and whom I assume to have been the Privy Councillor of
that name appointed in 1783, was the draughtsman of the
instrument of the *Fürstenbund*, which under his hand assumed
the character of a vindication of State rights against the
encroachments of a would-be centralising authority.

   After the death of the great King, the British desire for
a friendly understanding with Prussia was met halfway from
Berlin, so long as the Friderician traditions were maintained
there by Hertzberg.   Indeed, under Frederick William II
this good understanding progressed as far as a new Triple
Alliance between Great Britain, Prussia, and the repentant
Provinces ; and wider schemes were entertained, with the aid
of which the gauntlet might once more have been thrown
down to a Russo-Austrian Alliance.   But the younger Pitt
shrank from these proposals, which involved the separation
from the *nexus* of the Austrian dominions of an independent
Belgium, completing the arch of a great Maritime Alliance
of which Hanover would, so to speak, have been the
keystone.   Isolated in her turn, Prussia now definitively
exchanged the friendship of Great Britain for that of
Austria; with whom at Reichenbach (1790) she entered
into an understanding concerning Poland and against
Revolutionary France.   A new era begins in the history
of Europe.

   The Coalition fell to pieces in 1795, when, in the Peace of

------

[1] In *Die deutschen Mächte und der Fürstenbund*, one of the most
instructive, I venture to think, of the great historian's minor works.

Bâle, Prussia sacrificed the left bank of the Rhine, but was in one secret article promised compensation elsewhere, while another imposed neutrality upon the North German territories beyond a certain line of demarcation. These territories included Hanover, and Prussia undertook, in the event of Hanover refusing to accept this neutrality, to occupy the Electorate as a pledge. With these arrangements begins that long and lamentable episode in the history of the Personal Union which still awaits the pen of an unbiassed historian. In the present connexion it must suffice to affirm that during the whole of this period Hanover was helpless in the hands whether of neighbours or of strangers, and that Great Britain was impotent to protect her against either.

The first Prussian occupation of the Electorate (March, 1801) had for its pretext certain offences—whether actual or fictitious is of little consequence—on the part of Great Britain against the Armed Neutrality of the North. It was really due in part to the direct suggestion of France, in part to the fear of Prussia, that she might be anticipated by Russia—though it was continued even after the policy of Russia had been reversed by the death of Paul I—partly, however, and chiefly, to the desire of Prussia to make sure of the territorial compensation which had remained unsettled at Lunéville. It lasted for about seven months; it cost the country more than a million of dollars; it proved of no advantage to the occupying Power; and it sowed in the Hanoverian population a distrust of that Power which endured for generations.

The first Prussian occupation had come to an end a few weeks after the preliminaries of peace had been signed between Great Britain and France in October, 1801. When in May, 1803, war broke out again between those two Powers, the doom of Hanover was sealed, and although the calamities which ensued were shared by her with the greater part

of Germany at large, the circumstances of the Personal Union
aggravated her sufferings, while throwing upon Great Britain
a responsibility which, with all her resources and all the
strength of will that left her victorious at the last, she was
unable to meet.

No incident in this period of humiliation furnishes a more
striking proof of this inability than the catastrophe with which
the French occupation of the Electorate in the years 1803–5
opened. Indeed, had a narrative of these events been possible
on the present occasion, it would have formed a sequel—
strangely close in some respects, though fortunately not in
all—to the story of Kloster Zeven [1]. In the spring of 1803
it was still uncertain whether peace would after all be
preserved between France and Great Britain; but no doubt
whatever remained that, should this not be the case, France
would fall upon Hanover. The Hanoverian Government
had been informed by King George that an application to
Prussia for assistance seemed in the first instance desirable,
but that if the Privy Council preferred not to act on this
suggestion, it would be advisable to draw away the Hanoverian army to Stade (the route taken by the Duke of
Cumberland after Hastenbeck) and to ship it thence to
England. The Hanoverian Government, for reasons which
it is impossible but to approve, declined to adopt the
former alternative. It has been severely blamed for not
having responded to the second suggestion, and thus added
15,000—or rather perhaps 30,000—men to the military
force at the disposal of the British Crown, while leaving
Bonaparte to inflict such reprisals as he chose upon the

---

[1] The most accessible English account of the events briefly noticed in
the text is to be found in N. L. Beamish's *History of the King's German
Legion* (1832); the Hanoverian authorities, including the Field-Marshal's
own Apologies, are cited in the article on Wallmoden in vol. xl. of
the *Allgemeine Deutsche Biographie*.

population of the Electorate. The blame which the Hanoverian Privy Council really deserves is neither for commission nor for omission, but for a hopelessly fatal dilatori-
ness. Field-Marshal Wallmoden, who was in command of
the Hanoverian troops, may technically not have rendered
himself amenable in the same measure to the same charge ;
as a matter of fact, however, his irresolution materially contributed to the final result. Thus, the Sovereign sent no
orders ; the Commander-in-Chief declined to take the responsibility of providing for the defence of the country ; and the
population was divided between apprehensions of invasion,
and the fear of a military levy which would entail more certain
if less extended hardships. While the French were already
massing their regiments on the Dutch frontier under the title
of *l'armée d'Hanovre*, the Hanoverian Privy Council had only
reached the point of directing that the numbers of the army
should be increased and a camp of instruction set up. From
London Wallmoden was apprised that he and the Government
must act according to circumstances—repulse the enemy,
defend the country, secure a favourable position for the army,
embark it, capitulate. Even then, had the weakness and bad
equipment of the French force been known to the Hanoverians, the most humiliating of these several courses might
have been avoided. But the soldiery were disheartened, all trust
in either Government or Commander was at an end, and when
the French army actually advanced upon the Weser, and
General Mortier announced the First Consul's demand that
the whole of the Hanoverian troops should withdraw beyond
the Elbe and lay down their arms, this demand was transmitted
to the Privy Council and accepted by it. The Suhlingen
capitulation having been signed, the march—a series of hardships and humiliations—commenced. The French were on
the heels of the bewildered troops, and it was with difficulty
that they managed to cross the Elbe. On the further side of

the river the tidings reached Wallmoden that the First Consul
had refused to approve of the capitulation, until (he was not
likely to have forgotten Kloster Zeven) he should have been
informed of its ratification by King George III. When the
King's answer arrived, it insisted with incontrovertible logic
upon the principle that—to quote Lord Hawkesbury's words—
he ought not to be held liable in one country for a line of
conduct which he might have felt it his duty to adopt in the
other. He therefore contented himself with appealing to
the Empire in the matter of the violation of his electoral
dominions ; but, in order no doubt to save the unhappy
army from further complications, he undertook in the mean-
time to do nothing in contravention of the capitulation of
Suhlingen. In accordance with its formal terms rather than
its obvious intention, and in deference to the First Consul's
manifest wish to see the Electorate as a conquered country
at his feet, King George's answer was treated as a refusal
to ratify. Wallmoden, who was by no means wanting in
personal courage—although he had no Guelph blood in his
veins, he was closely connected with the electoral family—
would even now have risked a conflict in arms. But a
mutiny broke out among his troops, which he was unable to
suppress, and in the end he was forced to conclude a second
convention (the so-called Elbe Convention), which was a copy
of that of Suhlingen. The Hanoverian army was hereupon
disbanded. It would be short-sighted to blame the British
Government for the radically false conditions of a Union
which was no union, and which it could only be to the dis-
advantage of both partners to attempt to treat as if it had
been such, but of which an enemy like Bonaparte was certain
to make the most. And it was to their credit that they did
their best to temper the cruel absurdity of a situation which
they had not themselves created. But the dishonour of the
double capitulation remained, and neither Great Britain nor

Hanover escaped their respective shares of it. It is distasteful to be obliged to add that the unsoundness of the basis of the Personal Union made itself perceptible even in the arrangements for the honourable bond which after the capitulation was established between the British and the Hanoverian armies, and of which the remembrance will never be effaced from the minds of patriotic Englishmen. The history of the German Legion fills many honourable, and some glorious pages, in the annals of the British army; and one would willingly allow the high deserts of this association to cover a dubious passage in the record of its beginnings. The Convention of Suhlingen had been acted upon so precipitately that no time had been left to place on their parole the great body of the troops whom it subjected to the condition of not bearing arms against France in the course of a war actually renewed only a fortnight before; and the second or Elbe Convention was never formally made known to the soldiers, of whom many had already taken their departure from the army. The King of Great Britain, having never accepted the second convention, may be held to have acted within his rights in declaring, as he did in the following month (July), that the Hanoverian troops were free from any obligation to observe it, and in issuing letters of service for the raising of a foreign corps primarily designed as an inducement to the disbanded Hanoverians to enlist as British soldiers. A free passage through Holstein granted by the Danish Government greatly facilitated a response to these invitations, and in October was formed the King's German Regiment, in the first instance under the command of Major von Hinüber—at times there is something in a name. Such was the origin of the distinguished corps, which under its subsequent designation of the German Legion, on many a hard-fought field of the Peninsula, in other varied service, and finally at Quatrebras and Waterloo, intertwined the laurels gained by its gallant combatants with those of their British comrades in arms, and will with them remain unforgotten.

I would gladly break off on this note, but historical veracity demands a different kind of conclusion. Hanover, as Häusser reminds us in one of those outbursts of generous indignation which animate the masterpiece of this truly patriotic historian [1], was the German territory which first experienced the iron rule of the conqueror, destined to lie so heavy and so long—as it seemed even to that sorely-tried and patient age—upon the greater part of Germany. This infliction, although directly attributable to the pusillanimity of the native authority, which like many another oligarchy under the strain of peril had proved incapable of the impetus often leading to unexpected success, had been essentially due to Hanover's connexion with the great Maritime Power.

Neither the right nor the left arm of that Power, although stretching across two hemispheres, was of avail to defend the involuntary partner of her destinies, upon whose shores her own looked across the German Ocean. During the French occupation which ensued, the Hanoverian Privy Council split into two sections,—the one continuing as a sort of administration *in partibus* at Schwerin, the other remaining *incognito* at Hanover, and there carrying on a sort of secret control of the Government in conjunction with the ministers beyond the Elbe. In all this there was so much of mere playing at government that one can hardly wonder at the indifference felt in London as to consulting either Schwerin or Hanover, or at the orders finally sent to the electoral representatives and agents to report directly to the London Chancery. The appointment of Münster in 1805 practically put an end to the melancholy endeavours at galvanising an extinct authority. Meanwhile, in the Electorate, the French seemed at first

---

[1] *Deutsche Geschichte vom Tode Friedrichs des Grossen* (edn. 1862), vol. i. p. 464.

single-mindedly intent upon extracting and extorting as much
as they could from the population, repeating on a more ex-
tensive scale, and with a slighter admixture of the amenities
of which even war admits, the oppressive proceedings under
which the country had suffered in the days of the Seven
Years' War. The invading army, besides being quartered on
the inhabitants, was paid out of their taxes; its cavalry was
remounted, and its general equipment renewed. Thus families,
municipalities, and the State were alike plunged into debt;
and the calculation has been made that during the twenty-six
months of the French occupation in question, it cost at least
as many millions of dollars to the Electorate, whose ordinary
revenues were reckoned *per annum* at less than one-fifth of
this total. In reply to deputations, Bonaparte expressed his
wish that the French name should be beloved among the
Hanoverians, and ordered a certain reduction in the army
of occupation; but it was not till June, 1804, that the
treatment of the unlucky country was mitigated by Mortier's
successor Bernadotte.

In 1805, when the Third Coalition set on foot by Pitt had
been called into life, and Napoleon, having abandoned his
project of invading England, turned against Austria, the
armies of the French Empire were set in motion towards
the Rhine; and among them that of Hanover under Bernadotte quitted the Electorate. It was at once occupied by
Russians, Swedes, and the German Legion of the King of
Great Britain, of which many officers and soldiers were
thus unexpectedly brought back for the moment to their
native land. For a short space of time—something under
two months—the authority of George III was again established in the Electorate, the control of military affairs being
by proclamation vested in the Duke of Cambridge, while
Count Münster was directed to report on the condition of
the civil administration, and to provide for immediate require-

ments. The recovery of Hanover, the principal object of
the important treaty negotiated by Münster at St. Petersburg
which had formed the foundation of the Third Coalition,
thus seemed accomplished; but the hope of drawing Frederick
William III of Prussia into the Coalition became fainter and
fainter, while Talleyrand's honest brokerage offered Hanover
to Prussia as the price of a counter-alliance with France.
We must pass by the negotiations which ensued between Great
Britain and Prussia on the subject of an entire or partial cession
of Hanover, when in the autumn of 1805 Prussia was on the
point of joining the Coalition against Napoleon. They
were scattered by the sun of Austerlitz; and after, in January,
1806, her troops had provisionally occupied Hanover, Prussia
in April formally entered into possession of the Electorate
as ceded by France, who had held it by right of con-
quest. In June Great Britain declared war against Prussia.
The author of the elaborate manifesto, in which King
George III reviewed and reprobated the policy of Prussia,
was Count Münster, whom Hardenberg upbraided for refusing
to recognise that Hanover's salvation lay in annexation to
Prussia. The argument had in it much that was weighty;
but it was out of season. Hanover was the price paid by
France for the offensive and defensive alliance of Prussia.
When, a few months later, this alliance ended in war and
disaster, the unfortunate Electorate fell back into the foreign
conqueror's grasp. After the catastrophe of Jena (October
14, 1806), Hanover was at once reoccupied by the French,
under the command of the General Mortier who had headed
the earlier occupation, and who was not likely to be stopped
by the placards bearing the device 'Neutral Territory,'
substituted for the Prussian eagles by the native authorities.
The land remained under French domination till the War
of Liberation, from 1810 onwards forming part of the
kingdom of Westphalia—a feebly rather than viciously ruled

pachalik; for poor King Jerome was not so much as the master of his secret police.

During all the years of hostile occupation, the Government in London had sought to maintain some sort of connexion with the Electorate; but this had of necessity been fitful and ineffective. On the other hand, Count Münster, who in 1805 had permanently succeeded Baron Lenthe as the Hanoverian minister in London, during the same period exercised a political influence in the affairs of Europe, which in its ubiquity recalls that of Bernstorff and Bothmer in the days of George I, and in its sustained personal authority that of Münchhausen under George II, and in the earlier years of George III. Münster stood in the centre of European diplomatic activity, holding a unique position among the politicians of this troubled age by virtue of his intimate knowledge of continental affairs. The trust continuously reposed in him by the King and the Prince Regent secured to him the attention of both British and Continental statesmen, and the patriotic spirit which, besides animating his official activity, kept him in private touch with the great European movement of resistance against the Napoleonic despotism, and in particular with such representatives of that movement as Stein and Gneisenau. The Hanoverian envoys in Berlin and Vienna, although their official occupation had gone, remained in residence there and kept him well informed;—it was through him, for instance, that the great design of Austria to declare war against Napoleon in 1809 became known to the British Government. In the same year Münster, with whom Canning was in agreement on this head, strongly urged that the enterprise which has acquired a melancholy title to remembrance under the name of the Walcheren expedition, should be directed to the Hanoverian coast, with a view to the liberation of the Electorate from the French yoke. Seeley calls Münster the

Metternich of the smaller German States; but there seems little force in the simile.

At the Congress of Vienna in 1814–5, it fell to Münster's lot, as representing Hanover, to guard in the first instance the immediate interests of .his native land; and it was no doubt due to his personal influence among the diplomatists assembled at the Congress, as well as to Great Britain's commanding position in Europe, that Hanover issued forth from the Congress increased by about one-fifth of its previous size, at last in the possession of the East Frisian coast-line, and raised to the dignity of a kingdom. Of his exertions at the Congress, and more especially of his opposition to those schemes for the reorganisation of Germany, which would have led to the establishment of a Prussian hegemony over Northern Germany, this is not the place to speak[1]. He would have preferred to any other scheme the restoration of the old Empire, of course under Austrian headship; and in the acute conflict between the two German Powers which arose on the subject of the fate of Saxony, he ranged himself with his British colleagues on the Austrian side. But something beyond jealousy of Prussia attracted the sympathy of Münster to a scheme of which the authorship was at one time assigned to him, but is now known to have been submitted to the Prince Regent by Gneisenau during his memorable visit to Linden at the close of the year 1812. With Gneisenau, as Pertz says, the scheme was a means to an end—a British expedition to Germany; with Münster, who had entertained similar proposals before Gneisenau's earlier visit to London, and discussed them with members of the English royal family, it was an end in itself[2]. This end was,

[1] His reports to the Prince Regent were published as an Appendix to a slight volume of political reflexions by Count Münster's son (Leipzig, 1867).

[2] See Pertz, *Gneisenau*, vol. ii. pp. 439 seqq.; and cf. *ib., Appendix*, p. 674.

in a word, the formation of a large Low German State, reaching from the mouth of the Elbe to that of the Schelde, which in the expected event of the British throne passing into the female line should, under a male descendant of Henry the Lion, in some measure revive his territorial power on Germanic soil. However, the opportunity of initiating such a policy, if it ever existed, passed with the course taken by the war which led to the settlement of the Congress of Vienna. And in lieu of a great Guelphic Austrasia, the new kingdom of Hanover remained planted midway between the two divisions of Prussia—a position ominous of future trouble, whether or not the dynastic connexion between Great Britain and Hanover continued. The Congress separated without the influence of Münster or Hanover having contributed to any satisfactory national settlement of the German question. In the mercantile difficulty as to the freedom of the great North German rivers, the particular interests of Hanover ranged her on the side of obstruction, from which British interests in their turn were not strong or vigilant enough to detach her.

So long as the ultimate succession of the Princess Charlotte to the British throne seemed assured, the first condition of the interesting scheme or dream to which I have referred seemed sure sooner or later to become a fact, and the Personal Union certain to find its natural end. For the last time the historic connexion between Great Britain and Hanover was brought home to the populations of both countries by the battles of Quatrebras and Waterloo ; and then, under circumstances which unfortunately once more illustrated the inherent defects of a system of divided interests [1], the German Legion was dis-

---

[1] The existing Hanoverian army, which had taken its share in the brief War of Liberation, held its interests to be imperilled by the proposed incorporation in it of the Legion, while the latter considered its claims as a distinguished veteran corps inadequately met.

banded (1815–6), and a memorable episode in the annals
of modern warfare came to a flat and painful conclusion.
Yet the history of the German Legion cannot in justice
be looked upon as a mere chapter in that of the mercenary system at large, of which Great Britain's policy of
intervention in the wars of Europe induced her to sustain
and protract the use.

Not in the way or at the time expected—not by the advent
to the British throne of the daughter of King George IV, but
by the much later accession of Her present Gracious Majesty—
the Union was in the end dissolved. Herein at least both
countries were fortunate; for the event when it took place
had been long expected, and tacitly prepared. The two
countries had more and more drifted apart in their political
sentiments and aspirations[1]; and, except to courtiers, officials,

---

[1] It would serve no purpose to dwell on the changes effected
during the remaining years of the Personal Union in the constitution
and administrative system of the kingdom of Hanover. They were
due to the popular movement which agitated Germany in the period
ensuing on the War of Liberation, and were facilitated by the docile
ambition of the Duke of Cambridge, against which Münster was
ultimately unable to prevail. In 1816 he had addressed himself to
the reorganisation of the internal administration of the new kingdom,
and practically remained at its head till 1831. Then, however, after the
accession of William IV to the British throne, advantage was taken of
an agitation for reform, which at this epoch made itself felt everywhere,
to bring about a series of changes including the elevation of the Duke of
Cambridge from the dignity of Governor-General to that of Viceroy,
under conditions which removed certain of the restrictions previously
imposed upon his authority, and Münster was dismissed. Proposals
were at the same time brought forward for a revision of the Constitution which in 1819 had been bestowed upon Hanover, but which had
made little actual difference in the system of government, and had been
accepted without much emotion by the population. The new Constitution
was in 1833 finally sanctioned by King William, but unfortunately it
was omitted to obtain the assent of the heir-presumptive to the throne,
the Duke of Cumberland. Thus when, four years later, he actually

and military veterans, the Personal Union had come to seem little more than a name even while it still continued to be a fact. The problem had ceased to be a problem since it had sunk into a mere question of the revolving years; and, in the end, two populations to whose burdens and troubles their involuntary connexion had in divers ways and proportions added, once more fell asunder. It mattered little that they were akin in descent, and had in common not a few physical, mental, and moral features. On the one side the use made of the opportunities of the Union for dynastic ends was with constant violence, but not always wholly without cause, decried as prejudicial to important national interests. On the other, the same tie came very slowly, but very surely, to be recognised as having retarded an enduring association with the fortunes of the German people, and with the future to which it was looking forward. On neither side is the lesson brought home to it likely to be forgotten. The great efforts and achievements in which Great Britain and Hanover each had a share should nevertheless remain for both countries a historic remembrance of unusual interest, and the foundations of a lasting mutual good will.

succeeded to the Hanoverian throne, a constitutional conflict could hardly fail to ensue, and he was not the man to avoid it. But with the whole of these transactions British policy neither had nor affected any concern.

INDEX

OF PRINCIPAL NAMES AND TOPICS

THE END